# Speaking for Ourselves

# Speaking for Ourselves

## VOICES OF BIBLICAL WOMEN

Katerina Katsarka Whitley

MOREHOUSE PUBLISHING
HARRISBURG, PENNSYLVANIA

Copyright © 1998 by Katerina Katsarka Whitley

**Morehouse Publishing**
P.O. Box 1321
Harrisburg, PA 17105

Morehouse Publishing is a division of The Morehouse Group.

Printed in the United States of America

Cover art: Jewish Museum, New York/SuperStock. *Ruth Takes Away the Barley* by James J. Tissot.

Cover design by Trude Brummer

**Library of Congress Cataloging-in-Publication Data**

Whitley, Katerina Katsarka.
    Speaking for Ourselves : voices of biblical women / Katerina Katsarka Whitley.
        p.    cm.
    Includes bibliographical references.
    ISBN 0-8192-1758-1 (pbk.)
    1. Women in the Bible.    I. Title.
BS575. W533    1998
220.9'2'082—dc21                                                98-38339
                                                                        CIP

*To Dorothy L. Sayers and C. S. Lewis,*
*and to DeWitt Myers and Rudy Whitley—*
*all guides to the Light*

# Contents

# Acknowledgments

I am grateful to all the parishes and women's groups that have invited me to present some of these monologues in the place of a sermon or on other occasions, and to the rectors who offered me the pulpit, especially to the Reverend Judson Mayfield, who first said that Mary's monologues belong within the celebration of the Eucharist. The reaction of the listeners filled me with surprise and awe, and convinced me that I should make these available to readers and to other interpreters of the Word.

It is difficult to thank all the writers who influenced me in my understanding of these women of the Bible. Eternal gratitude to my father, who read the Bible to me when I was too young to know anything but the feeling the stories created in me of beauty, terror, sacrifice, and love. To Dorothy L. Sayers and all the writers and teachers who helped me emerge from the literal reading of the Bible into the light and terror of biblical criticism, I owe many thanks.

I want to thank Marilyn Bentov, Ph.D., for teaching me the meaning of the midrash. "Miriam's Secret" was written in her class as a midrash exercise.

The Syrophoenician woman's contribution to Jesus' understanding of his mission to the rest of the world, not just "to the children of the house of Israel," I owe to Bishop Bennett Sims, who preached on this story in Anaheim, during the 1985 General Convention of the Episcopal Church, and caused me to look at her with new eyes.

My son-in-law, Kenneth Craig, Ph.D., with his love and knowledge of the Old Testament, helped me see the women with a deeper understanding of the historical circumstances surrounding them.

My friend Linda Chamberlain, who heard me read the first monologue, "To a Poor Girl, Such Promises!" and asked with enthusiasm, "Do you know what a strong feminist story this is?" gave me the idea to explore this liberation theme in the lives of other biblical women.

And to my two daughters, Niki and Maria, I owe the warmest thanks for teaching me the wonder, awe, and tender love (storgé) of motherhood. They have made all the mothers in the Bible known to me.

# Introduction

The women of the Bible. They are friends who are always with me. They come to me during the night, and in the daytime, and I listen to them. They speak their stories to me; and I have recorded them in the monologues of this book. I say this not as a mystic, but as one who loves these women for their humanity. They come to tell me their stories. And I, an avowed Protestant, an Episcopalian thoroughly immersed in Scripture, am bold enough to admit that I owe it all to the Virgin Mary.

I was born in Greece. Yet, I was a rather strange Greek. I did not grow up in the Greek Orthodox tradition. As a result, my evangelical family and I missed much of the beauty and, what seemed to us, the slight lunacy of that tradition that is overloaded with saints. We ignored the Virgin Mary and all the saints with a zealous, deliberate, Reformation-inspired indifference. My fascination with the Virgin Mary came later, in my middle age, when I realized how much we evangelicals had thrown away, frightened as we were of becoming infected with what my father called "the sin of Mariolatry" (Mary worship). He explained to us that our nonevangelical compatriots were Orthodox Christians only by birthright. They did not read the Bible for themselves, so they did not realize that they had elevated Mary to the status of the divine. And, as children, we accepted this. Later, when I realized that language reveals history and culture, I was convinced. The Greek language is full of exclamatory phrases that pepper every conversation and storytelling. Let me explain.

A Greek woman, when confronted with something sad or joyful, will exclaim, *"Ach, Panayía mou!"* (Oh, my All-Holy-One!). The ending of this phrase is understood to be feminine, and there is only one Pán-áyia, one "all-holy" woman for the Greeks—the Virgin Mary, the mother of Jesus. In the tradition of those who are greatly loved, her name and all her titles are used in the Greek language for exclamations as well as, unfortunately, for major blasphemies.

Her name as "Panayía," never as Maria, is taken in vain constantly, but a Greek will pray to her before she ever thinks of praying to God or to Jesus. Jesus is usually *Christoúlis*—little Christ. In the Greek lexicon and in popular religion, he has never reached the stature of his mother.

However, in a country long steeped in the worship of women, this is not at all strange. Athená, the goddess of wisdom, the protector of the Athenians and all Greeks, was pictured and sculpted as fully armed, with a helmet, javelin, and shield. Homer's writings are full of Athená's help to the Greeks, especially to the crafty Odysseus, and there are testimonials of her fighting alongside the Greek armies. Likewise, in 1940, twenty-eight centuries after Homer, soldiers returning from the Albanian front, where the ragged Greek army defeated the Italians of Mussolini, described how they had seen the Virgin Mary, fully armed, leading them on to victory. Every Greek child has heard these stories, and for people like me, who were children during the war, the memories are indelible.

In our evangelical home we grew up believing that a Christian must pray only to the one God, the Father of our Lord Jesus Christ, and to no one else. So I grew up ignoring Maria, the mother of Jesus, because I did not want to fall into Mariolatry. But by the time I became the mother of two daughters, occasionally paralyzed by the fear of something terrible happening to my children, I was ready to rethink my attitude toward the mother of Jesus. In doing so, I was helped tremendously by the writings of Dorothy L. Sayers and her marvelous cycle of plays, *The Man Born to Be King.* Her plays, which I read in the seventies and used during Lent as the basis for a reader's theater in my home parish, radically changed my Christian understanding. For the first time, Jesus and his mother, and his friends and disciples, became living, breathing human beings throbbing with life and pain, sorrow and laughter. The incarnation became the central focus of my faith, and Mary became for me the girl, the woman, and the mother I had neglected. I was ready to listen to her.

She came to me as a mother and, because that spoke to what was and is most precious to my heart, I heard her. Her talking about the birth of her child and the wondrous circumstances surrounding it made her so real and so fully human that I felt as though a door had opened that led to light. Beyond that door I saw much that I would call joy, but also great pain. I wondered, if she can talk about this child with so much promise born in such strange surroundings, what was she remembering at the foot of the cross? What happened to that promise?

And what about all the other women who come to us through the stories, but usually only in tantalizing hints? What would they say? I remembered all the Old Testament stories that I had heard as a child, when my father read us a portion of Scripture every single night of our childhood years, even those years when we had no electricity because of the German occupation of Greece. I can still see his dear face as he bent over his Bible and we sat around the table listening, our shadows long and mysterious on the walls, the soft light of the lamp, my young self full of emotion and questions. *Why are these women punished and not the men? Why do some of these stories make me so sad?* Underlining all the marvelous stories was Daddy's assurance that all this was inspired by God, that there was nothing false and nothing wrong in the Bible. Yet, his explanations of faith and obedience didn't always satisfy me.

When I was in college, in America, and under the influence of the writings of C. S. Lewis and several beloved professors, the mantle of inerrancy fell from the stories. This was liberating for me, as it has been for countless believers who have emerged from fundamentalism. (I no longer felt obligated to believe in an Old Testament God who ordered babies to be dashed against the walls and who punished Saul because he did not utterly destroy his enemies.) It is difficult for people who have not been brought up as fundamentalists to realize the freedom that comes with the understanding that the *writers* wrote down these stories; they were not *dictated* by God. The stories reveal the level of understanding of the divine that the people of the time had reached, rather than God's absolute truth written in stone.

When the time came for me to listen to the women, I was ready to hear them because I had shed the notion that they had acted in the way they did because they were foreordained to do so. I knew then that their stories were not written down by inerrant writers hearing the word of God directly, but by human beings who saw them in a particular light—that of their own faith, inspired by God but also inspired by misconceptions and the limited understanding of a man-centered culture.

I wondered about the writers of the Bible who wrote about the women, some in remarkably vivid stories, like those of Miriam and Tamar, and others only in passing, like the mention of Lydia or Gomer. What was going on? Why did the writers choose these stories? Given the status of women in biblical times, I was amazed that the writers did not totally ignore such women but included them in the narration. What compelled them to write so much about women in a culture where only the men seemed to matter? Did these particular women leave such a strong memory behind that their stories could not be ignored? What was the oral tradition that kept their memories alive, and how did these stories influence the women who came after them? These are questions I longed to examine.

During the years of my travels for the Presiding Bishop's Fund for World Relief (the relief and development arm of the Episcopal Church), I came face-to-face with poverty and suffering—of women and children—that broke my heart and shook my faith in a loving God. I went back to Scripture to find out how the people within its pages dealt with questions that arose out of suffering, confusion, persecution, the mores of the times, and the prejudices and ignorance of the ancient world. I found in the women's stories much that sustained me and gave me strength to go on. It is these women, who gave me this strength, that you will meet in the monologues.

Each one of them visited me and spoke to me in her own way. These were not mystical experiences. Each monologue came out of reading the story, researching the related Scriptures, and then simply listening. Whenever I read about a woman in the Bible, I think, this is like shorthand. What else went on in this story? What is hidden here? These are a few of the questions I focus on, but above all I always ponder this one question: How would Lydia, Miriam, or Tamar tell this story in her own words? If any of them were interviewed by the writer, what would they remember? How would they express it? The personal story of each woman usually starts with a picture or with the first sentence playing itself in my mind. The rest comes easily. Since the time I first wrote about the Virgin Mary not as Theotokos, the mother of God, but as the wounded mother of a son who died young, I have not been able to read about any of the women in the

Bible without hearing their voices. And I have rejoiced in hearing them speaking for themselves.

I do not approach these monologues as a biblical scholar. Many others have conducted detailed, academic explorations of the women of the Bible. What I hope to do here is add the sound of these women's voices. I want their faithfulness, obedience, patience, strength, tenderness, and yes, even anger to shout and whisper through the words that were given to me. These monologues remain faithful to the biblical passages, but I have allowed my imagination to fill in the blanks.

I must stress that these stories arise from the whole panorama of Scripture, so it would be difficult to see them as part of a whole without some familiarity with both the Old and New Testaments. But the stories of these women can also be read singly, on a very intimate, personal level. So at the beginning of each monologue I have given the passages that pertain to the person telling the story. You may want to read the scriptural passages after you read the monologue. Reading them in a variety of different biblical translations may be illuminating. But don't stop there. Search the chapters that come before and after, and you will be surprised by new insights simply because the story is told from a different perspective. A few women's groups have used the Mary monologues as springboards for discussion in examining their own spirituality. I was so impressed by their comments that I decided to add questions at the end of each chapter for discussion. I hope you will find them helpful.

These monologues are written to be read aloud. Even when you are alone, read them aloud and hear the voices.

What wealth of spiritual courage these women show.
What instinctive understanding of the divine in their
lives. Thanks be to God for them.

## A Note on the Use of Names

I know that the use of Luke as the interviewer/listener in
the monologues of the gospel women is probably not
correct chronologically. However, I chose him for his
understanding and kind treatment of women. I wanted a
sympathetic listener, and Luke fits the role beautifully.

I have stayed with the pronunciation of the names
found in the English translations of the Bible, except for
places where the Greek version made more sense because
the names are called by the speaker. Therefore, I have
chosen to use the Greek version of the names for Mary
(Mariam), Mark (Markos), and Peter (Petros).

## A Word about Dramatic Monologues

Poetic dramatic monologues had a powerful influence in
my life, and for that I owe thanks to Robert Browning and
Professor R.N. Daniels of Furman University, who
revealed Browning to me during a very impressionable
semester of study when I was nineteen years old.

The dramatic monologues of Browning reveal character, and the drama in them, expressed only through the
voice of the reader, strengthened my conviction that this
was the best way for me to communicate the good news
of God to others. My professors of speech and drama
encouraged me in this.

So I studied what Browning did with his monologues and used portions of them in many of my own speeches. My faith in the incarnation was enlarged by Browning's own magnificent affirmations at the end of some of his finest dramatic poems: "Kashish the Arab Physician," "Cleon," and "Saul." In them, the speaker tells the story to a listener who never speaks but influences the course of the monologue with his silences or looks or even questions that no one else hears. Using only a few words, Browning lets us enter into the culture of that day, the speaker's psyche, and the poet's own convictions. So these monologues have many layers and subtleties.

# To a Poor Girl, Such Promises!

## MARY REMEMBERS THE COMING

**All of the Gospel of Luke, specifically 1:26–56; 2:1–52
Matthew 1:18–25; 2:1–11**

*(The speaker is Mariam, the mother of Jesus, and the listener
is the evangelist Luke.)*

Yes, Brother Luke, I'll answer your questions gladly. Do sit with me a while then. Talking about his early years is my only comfort now. He has been gone from earth a long while. I miss the child he was. My old heart warms at the memory of his sweetness.

And you will write a book about him, you say, so you want "perfect understanding of all things from the very first"? Yes, I will help you. You are a learned man, beloved physician. They tell me your Greek is beautiful—you are a master of the language. But you must try to think like a Jew to understand me. Yes, write your book. Very few know his early years; even Markos[1] did not touch upon

---

1. The birth narratives are found only in Matthew and Luke. The earliest written gospel, Mark, did not refer to the stories she is telling Luke.

them. Nobody really asked about them for a long while—not after the horror of the cross, and then the glory.

Let me warn you, I drift easily these days; my years are long. Soon I, too, will go to the Father. My days are numbered. Do not let me sleep. You are a busy man.

Where shall I begin? (*She listens to Luke's question.*)

What did I think of during those days? The strange, scary birth, the smelly stable, and my beloved Joseph, all alone with no one to help him. Was I scared? Beloved physician! You know your science well, but you have never given birth. So how shall I explain? With all my other children, the pains seemed the same. But with him, the firstborn, even the pains were different; as though less eager was he to enter the world, yet more alive when he came than any infant I have ever seen.

A few hours before his birth, exhausted after the long journey from Nazareth, looking at Joseph, who could not find a room in the inn, and seeing his agony, I had wept at our aloneness. *Was this the favor God had shown me?* But afterward, when the Babe in my arms wept to enter this world, then lifted up his little hand and touched my own hot tears, I felt that rest, the peace that passes understanding, that our poets have sung about.

And soon the shepherds came in, and we were no longer alone, but rejoiced in their company. I see you heard of the shepherds? Did one of them tell you? There was a lad among them. Perhaps he's living still . . . (*Pauses, listening to Luke.*)

And now you ask if *they* were frightened when they saw the angels. Have you ever seen an angel, Brother Luke? No? Then how shall I describe to you the awesome aspect? The shiny, holy quality of these servants who stand before our Lord? You want to fall on your knees, to hide your face from the brightness. *(In awe)* When the Blessed Gabriel appeared to me, the trembling in my soul lasted for days. And long afterward, my eyes deep inside hurt from the light that seared me to the soul.

So I knew the shepherd's fear when the angel appeared to them that night. It is a good kind of fear, you understand, a holy thing. I knew from their eyes when they crowded into the stable that they had been in the presence of that brightness. Wordless at first, they looked for a sign, the swaddling clothes, and among them they found the Babe. So they fell on their knees, and then their tongues were loosened, and they spoke and sang at the same time. Then they told us of the angels' words to them . . .

You want to know what they were? I'm almost hesitant to tell you. How did we all forget them so soon? Thirty-three years later there was no hint of all that glory—not with him hanging broken on a cross. We all stood hopeless, away from him; even I, his mother, had forgotten the angels' words and had no hope, no hope . . .

*(Her tone changes from sadness to remembered sweetness.)*

But that first night in Bethlehem the shepherds told us, and we all believed them. "I bring you good news," the angel told the shepherds, "good news of a great joy which will come to all people. For to you is born a Savior . . . " *(With amazement)* Can you imagine? An angel of the Lord revealing this great secret, the hope of Israel for generations, to the shepherds? And when they told us, I remembered Blessed Gabriel's words to me nine months earlier: "The child to be born will be called holy, the Son of God."

To the shepherds, and to a poor, unmarried girl, such promises . . .

But he did exalt the humble all that night. So lovely a night, Brother Luke. The manger smelled of springtime after his birth. The darkness was dissolved, and in that lowly stable shone the light of a holy presence.

It was a comforting light, not hot like the sun's, but silvery, like joy come alive. A light that sang entered the stable. Maybe it was an echo of the angels' song I heard, but the whole place was full of music. And I didn't even stop to wonder, is it possible that this baby in my arms is the Messiah of Israel? That night everything seemed possible, even peace on earth . . .

*(She drifts into a dream.)*

Ah, yes, I see I must have drifted away. It's easy to doze off at my age. Every time I think of that blessed night, I seem to leave the world.

Afterward, we moved to the house of one of the shepherds, who by then had offered us hospitality, embarrassed of the stable. In all our happiness, we lulled ourselves, Joseph and I, that we would enjoy the baby like normal parents and call him our own. I suckled him, held him, and changed him, loving him while Joseph fashioned a crib for him with his clever hands. The days passed in contentment, so that again Joseph and I forgot the strange apparitions in the night, the wonder and the prophecies.

But when we took him to the temple for the Presentation, an old sage by the name of Simeon, who was a prophet, brought the fear and the wonder back to my heart. He took my Jesus in his arms, his old face shattered in smiles and tears, and he said upon looking at my baby, he said: "Mine eyes have seen thy salvation, oh Lord." I knew, of course, that Jesus was not mine, but that he was a gift to all. Then Simeon's old eyes looked into my mind, and there was hard mercy in him as he said, "And a sword shall pierce your own soul also." I knew his meaning. I felt it suddenly in my heart: the horror of my life thirty-three years later.

And again we forgot, but then the Magi came in all their strange splendor and filled us both with foreboding. Different from the shepherds they were, ah yes. We were familiar with shepherds, had even become familiar—no, that is not the right word—had become used to the appearance of angels, but these visitors! They entered trailing many-colored robes, and sparkling with their jewels. They spoke strangely, they even smelled strange. Joseph looked lost. Up to then, he had been serene amidst the wondrous events of our lives, but in the presence of these Magi from the Orient, he became so confused, he stuttered.

Then one of the royal visitors approached me as I held my son, knelt, and uttered a great speech that I did not understand. Joseph, who knew some Greek, asked him the meaning of his words, and this kneeling prince of this world repeated them. "He is calling our Jesus King of the Jews!" Joseph explained in amazement. "How is it possible that these strangers know of the Messiah?"

But I was no longer surprised. It all fell into place—the words of Gabriel to me and to Joseph, the angels' words to the shepherds, and now the utterances of these wise men from the East. I again felt deep within me the knowledge and the light that were given to me upon that first visit from the angel. This baby Jesus was a gift of God for the whole world. Then I put this knowledge away until later, much later.

For immediately something happened that took from me the joy of the Lord and gave me the fear of a mother for her son. Our strange visitors knelt and offered gifts to the baby Jesus. There was a box of beautiful gold pieces, and my first thought was, lovely, I shall save it for him and he will not need to suffer want. I did not know then that the moment he was old enough to do so, he would give it all away to the poor. The other gifts were spices and perfumes. I still remember the pungent smell of frankincense permeating the room. But then one of them lifted a wreath of myrrh, and Jesus reach for it, grasped it, and put it on his head. And there was such a serious, intent look on that innocent face that a cold hand clutched at my heart when I smelled the bitter incense all over the lovely hair. Myrrh, I thought, myrrh for burial, my son. And I suddenly saw it as it happened thirty-three years later—the washing of his body and the anointing of it with myrrh . . .

Ah Luke, a sword pierced my heart that night in the presence of all the earthly wisdom of our visitors. Do you understand a mother's heart? What kind eyes you have; you must have known another's pain. Yes, I have grown weary, but I must finish, my young friend. You may not find me able to tell you again, so let me continue.

You asked what made him different from other children. Well, nothing really. He was childhood personified. All the joy and vivid energy of childhood were his: playfulness and curiosity and great generosity of spirit. Except for one thing, he was truly different. You see, I had other children by then and knew the difference.

Jesus was the only child I ever encountered who knew the meaning of total obedience. Do you know what that means? You nod but look bemused. How can I explain? When the day sang with its springtime promise and he longed to run outside to play or lie under a tree, all I had to do was look at him and say, "Help me with little James, my son. Look after him for me today." Jesus would stop at the door, turn around without regret, and do exactly as I asked, never once complaining.

And always, throughout the time he was with us, I wanted to spare him the suffering to come. I longed to keep him from pain. Let it come to me but not to him, I prayed, not to him. As though I knew that in this one desire of mine he would truly disobey me. I know now that there was no other way for the world to meet his perfect goodness. Only the cross. And soon he knew it.

But I have drifted from your questions. During those early years there were hints of both the glory and the pain, but they came more rarely. Soon he left home for good, without ever looking back. The rest you know. Blessed be the name of the Lord.

## Questions to Ponder

1. How has your understanding of Mary changed after reading this monologue?

2. The Greeks call Mary "Theotokos," the mother of God, or more accurately, "God-bearer." God chose

Mary, a woman of no previous importance, to bear Jesus, the Son of God. How does this knowledge shape your own understanding of God's ways of working in the world?

3. If an angel of God came to you and revealed the kinds of secrets he did to Mary, would you believe him? Would you do whatever you were asked to do?

4. In some religious traditions Mary is considered not only a virgin but sinless as well. Is this important to you? Why or why not?

5. Many mothers today, particularly those in inner cities and in war-torn parts of the world, must live with the realistic fear that their sons will not live a long life. How does Mary's courage speak to the realities of our violent world, where teenagers die at record rates?

# Was This the Promise God Had Given Me?

## MARY REMEMBERS THE LAST HOURS

**John 19:25–27; also, John 2:1–5**
**All of the Gospel of Luke**
**Matthew 1:18–25**
**Mark 3:31–35**
**Acts 1:14**

*(The speaker is Mariam, the mother of Jesus, and the listener is the evangelist Luke.)*

What broke on the cross that day, Brother Luke, was not his body only, but my heart.

I thought of Joseph. How he used to take a long piece of wood and, putting it across his knee, he'd break it in two with the pressure of his powerful hands. I said, "You broke me, Almighty. You broke me like a stick of kindling, and just as useless now."

For what sorrow can compare to a mother's sorrow? Seeing her son, her firstborn, dying on a tree, hanging there—that strong manly body hanging like a sack of

bones. Hanging by the hands whose very touch was healing itself—hands now bloodied and torn.

"They used to beg you for miracles, my son," I cried,
"and you never said no. No matter how tired you were,
you stretched out your hands and healed them. Do it
now, this one last time, for me, not for your sake but for
mine. Heal my heart; come down from that cross and
heal me."

*(Very quietly, the whole picture still vivid in her mind.)*

He didn't even look at me. He was absorbed in his own
terrible sorrow, and I didn't think it had to do with the
pain of his body. It was that distance that came over him
when he listened to his "Father," as he put it. But *that* day,
where was his Father? I think that his Father's absence
was behind his sorrow, and I knew it by the cries that
escaped him. So the abyss opened between us, and what
I remember now about that day is the darkness.

*(She remembers Luke's presence.)* What kind of darkness? Is that what you are asking? Ah, if I could only forget it . . . *(Runs her hands over her face.)*

You know how lovely our nights are in Galilee. The
light lingers and lingers and the dark comes softly, so you
still see faces with a sweet glow on them. And then the
stars are lit, low and so near and bright in the blessed sky.
It was nothing like that. That is the darkness *you* know.

This came suddenly, like the frightening storms over
the lake; it came with a groan, like an angry curse, and
covered everything with menace. The sun's light failed.

You look perplexed. It was the middle of the day, you
see, and the sun's light failed. I cringe to tell you what I

thought then. A good daughter of Judah doesn't think in such terms. "God is dead," I wailed, and it must have been at that moment that his soul left his body.

*(Pauses. Her voice changes, trying to become matter-of-fact, but as she describes the scene, it reaches a crescendo.)*

There was a crowd around the crosses, and the crazed Roman soldiers and all, but especially those Romans, were deathly frightened. The others, our own, were beating their breasts. They, who moments before were abusing him, were now running away with screams, asking God not to punish them for their evil deed. Curses and shameful words filled the air, and I don't know who was crying—maybe it was me—but I can still hear the lament.

"Blessed are the barren, and the wombs that never bore, and the breasts that never suckled." Later John told me that, because of the noise and fear, the crowds missed hearing the most loving words from the cross: "Father, forgive them," he had cried, "for they know not what they do." And all of us have been drawing comfort from that ever since.

But during those three hours the darkness was winning, and I kept remembering a psalm. I think I heard him cry it out, but John was leading me away by then, so as not to see the final agony. I remembered how Joseph used to teach him the Psalms. Once was enough—Jesus memorized them and delighted in them. He went about his chores repeating them, his lovely eyes with that secret light of understanding in them, full of their meaning, but *that* psalm made him so quiet. "*Eloi, Eloi, lama sabachthani*"; "My God, my God, why hast thou forsaken me?" he asked in pain and wonder, and I realized then that I had been asking the same thing. Why have you forsaken me, my son? That is when all abandoned the watch and turned in despair and fled. There was nothing left to live for.

*(She is recalled to the present.)*

But I am running ahead of my story. You see, Luke, I have not spoken of this to anyone in years.

Even the glory afterward did not diminish the pain of that day at the foot of the cross. Do you know that in moments of such terror and sorrow you remember so much of your life that you think eternity has passed? When I heard him cry out in thirst from the cross, I relived that day in Cana. You've heard of it? Well, it's all true. But what you don't know is that I went a-meddling. *(She smiles. This memory is pleasant.)*

I was so proud of him, and the wedding family were close friends. "Do something," I told him. "They have run out of wine." But what I really meant was: It is because of *you* that the place is running over with uninvited guests. They are the crowds that follow *you*.

But he only looked at me. Then he said, "My time has not yet come," and that's what I remembered under the cross. "Now," I cried, "now your time has come, and it is full of terror, and for *what?*"

And then it all came back to me. You and I have talked of this before, Luke, when I told you of his early years. But I didn't tell you that when Gabriel first appeared to me, I wanted to run and hide. For as soon as I said, "Let it be to me according to your word," I knew that one day it would lead to this. And my foolish heart asked, "What if I had said no to Gabriel, would it have ended differently?"

*(Her voice breaks.)* You see, my Brother Luke, it takes a lifetime to learn that we can't hide from the Almighty. We can't change him, and we can't stop him.

"And a sword shall pierce your own soul also," old Simeon had said, and I remembered. But I had not *ever* suspected it would be with this much pain.

*(She pauses. Listens to Luke's question and seems startled.)*

What, what is that you ask? Ah Luke, you ask such hard questions. Did I feel it was *my* son dying on that cross? I've told you this before. What hurt most bitterly during his lifetime was this—the knowledge that he wasn't my own. "You opened me up," my heart cried to the Lord. "You used me like a vessel, you emptied me, and then you threw me away and let him go his way, and he belonged to everyone but me."

It isn't an easy truth for a mother to bear. You want to know what helped? You will laugh, because it is so simple. It wasn't prayer, and it wasn't even the joy of his resurrection; it was John, my sweet, borrowed son. I left this for last because it is such a treasured moment.

As I told you, next to his pain the worst knowledge was that there was no hope. I begged for a quick death for him and for me. And then I heard his voice. "Woman," he said in that expression that always made me feel that I was all women and he honored them in me. "Woman, this is now your son," and he looked at John. "Ah," I cried, "you thought of me in the midst of your pain. I am not forsaken." And some of the burden lifted. "And this is now your mother," he told John, and that loving soul never forgot it. You see? *(She looks at Luke and waits.)* Well, not quite. Why should I assume that you understand what has taken me a lifetime to understand?

Remember, I confessed to you my lack of faith. I had thought that his death was for nothing and there was no hope. How did John change that? It came slowly. He became my family though I had other children. He was a good son though his own mother lived. And all along it was a secret he was revealing to me, but most of that is his story, and I know he will write it down one day. He has taught many of us to understand what Jesus said and did—me most of all—with great love and patience.

Dear John . . . Do you know that he and his brother James quarreled about being great chiefs in the kingdom Jesus would establish? Yes, yes, you wouldn't know it now, but John was ambitious. And then Jesus taught him, and all his dreams were turned inside out. He is now alone in exile—that loving, tender soul living all alone, pouring into letters his great love and joy. He who wanted to be in government lives all alone.

So I have learned the secret, and my world has turned upside down, too. I had wanted to obey the Lord, but to keep my son also. My son did not stay. Strangers became my sons.

Can you believe I was once fastidious? I used to dread the poor urchins he dragged in for me to clean and feed. Now lepers and poor and lame find their way to my home and I take them in. And no matter who they are, I say, "Welcome, Jesus, welcome, my child. Come in and let me serve you." This much I learned from John, and he learned it from his friend: to love the least of these. They are all my brothers and sisters, and they are all my Jesus.

(*With conviction*) No Luke, it was not for nothing that he died. He died for life. That is his gift. And it comes to each one of us a bit differently, but it comes. And the wonder is that it all makes good and holy sense, and, to a woman like me, that is of great value. Blessed be the name of the Lord.

## Questions to Ponder

1. On pages 22 and 23, Mary tells Luke: "For as soon as I said, 'Let it be to me according to your word,' I knew that one day it would lead to this. And my foolish heart asked, 'What if I had said no to Gabriel, would it have ended differently?' You see, my brother Luke, it takes a lifetime to learn that we can't hide from the Almighty. We can't change him, and we can't stop him." Do you think Mary could have said no to God? Do you believe that you can say no to God?

2. Mary has witnessed one of the most horrible things a parent can see—the cruel death of a child. Yet at the end of the monologue she can still say, "Blessed be the name of the Lord." Why do you think that Mary is still able to say this? What peace has she come to by the end of the monologue?

3. Why is Mary's focus on John so important? Did her love and gratitude for John come as a surprise to you? Why would the resurrection not be as comforting to her as is John's presence?

4. According to this monologue, Mary lived her whole life knowing that a sword would pierce her soul. What do you think gave Mary the courage to live her life anyway? What gives you the courage to live through difficult days?

5. Ultimately, did God do Mary a favor by choosing her to bear Jesus? Is she truly the favored one, as Scripture tells us? Why or why not?

# THREE

# Being Called by Name

## A WITNESS TO THE RESURRECTION

**Luke 8:2–3; 24:10**
**Matthew 27:56–61; 28:1, 9**
**Mark 15:40, 47; 16:1, 9**
**John: 19:25; 20:1, 11–18**

*(The speaker is Mary of Magdala, and the listener is the evangelist Luke.)*

It was the women I saw first, and I called out, "I've seen the Lord; he lives!" They peered at me for a moment, afraid I was mad with grief. But then they saw my joy, and they believed. They ran to the empty tomb and I went to tell his brethren, as Jesus had commanded me, for they were still in despair.

It is impossible for anyone outside the circle of the cross to comprehend the depth of our despair those days. What do I mean by the circle of the cross? The group that stayed with him to the end, when every hope was snatched from us, when it was crushed like the life that escaped his breast as he hung on that cross. Every hammer blow on his blessed hands and feet was a hammer blow that added to our pain.

We wept until you'd think the heart would hold no more tears. There is no loss that hurt as bitterly in all creation, because no life ever offered that much promise. So when he died, all promise and all hope died too. It was over.

But we stayed. We never left the circle—we, the women who had served him. *(With a bit of irony)* You see, we Hebrew women have learned to stay in the background; so probably our brethren did not notice and have not told you the whole story. There is shame in them that keeps them from telling you about us . . .

Who do you think fed all those men when they traveled with him from Capernaum to Nazareth, to Galilee, and, in the end, to Jerusalem? Who do you think cooked their meals and saw to it that they had clean tunics and cloaks to wear? And who do you think washed his feet when he stopped on those rare evenings to rest and be with us all, his family?

It was we, the women. His mother; Susanna; Mary and Martha of Bethany, Lazarus' sisters; and Joanna, whose husband had such a high position with Herod. But she gave it all up and traveled with us, and I, of course . . .

Why did we do it? Why . . . *(She tries to describe it.)*

Suppose you were drowning, and someone pulled you out and breathed life into you again. Would you not love him? Suppose darkness covered your mind until you thought the demons would devour you and he ordered them out of you; then light came and replaced the dark-

ness, and life was sweet again. Would you not then want
to live your life for him from that moment on?

What did he do for me? All that and more. Seven
demons pursued me—money and selfishness, and physi-
cal beauty that became so important that I was obsessed
with losing it. An illness in my soul that was both fear of
death and fear of life ate at me night and day until I was
incapable of laughter and joy. A deep depression covered
me, and I had left myself to die.

Joanna, who had been a childhood friend, took me to
hear him one day. Then, for the first time, I knew that I
wanted to live, just so I could see him again and hear him
again. It was then that the demons struggled to possess
me, afraid they could no longer have me, and he turned
and called me his own. "Leave her," he ordered. "She
belongs to me." And light flooded me.

I ran home long enough to sell my possessions, so that
all I had would be used to minister to him. I never left
him again. Not even at the foot of the cross, when all the
men, all the disciples, ran away. (*She listens.*)

Yes, you have the right to ask such a question, but you
don't understand. I was in despair when he died, but not
in the kind of darkness that covered me before I met him.
Once you have seen the light, you can never again go
willingly to the dark. No, no, this was different. I think
the women stayed to the end because Jesus had given us
a new life. He had shown us our true selves, so we knew
the power of our love and our strength. No matter that he
was dead, we were to stay near the body. That is simply
the way it is with women. We didn't even discuss it

among ourselves. We knew what was expected of us, and we did it.

The only one of the men who came back was John, but then John was always different from the rest—he was tender and loving like a woman—and that's why at the end Jesus entrusted his own mother to John.

So we watched until they took him down from the cross. Then I left him with his mother and the other women, and ran to get Joseph of Arimathea and Nicodemus—both good men, but hiding their loyalty because of the other Pharisees and teachers. They returned with me, with permission from Pilate to take care of the burial. Behind Golgotha was the garden with the tomb. They buried him there in Joseph's specially prepared burial place, and the guards rolled a heavy round stone in front of it. Then it was over. *(She listens to Luke's question.)*

Yes, the leaders had asked Pilate for guards. We could not understand it then. Were they afraid the body would walk away? Maybe they sensed something that we, in our sorrow, could not hope for . . .

We hid among the bushes and watched. We would not leave until the darkness came. Then, as soon as Sabbath ended, we went to the market long enough to get fresh linen and spices and perfumes to anoint the body. It was still dark, the first day. The others, exhausted, were looking after his poor, broken mother, but I could not rest away from him. I found my way back to the tomb, thinking of him behind that terrible stone that kept him in darkness, worrying about it. Could I find some friendly, strong men to roll it away, so that when the other women came we could wash his body and anoint it for proper burial?

And all the while my heart was heavy with the loss of hope. With my head as heavy as my heart, I approached the tomb and felt for the stone, but it wasn't there. By then, the dawn was breaking, and I saw that the tomb was empty. Without thinking, I ran to tell the others. I ran first to where the men were hiding. "They have taken the Lord out of the tomb," I told them. And before I had finished, Peter and John came out and were running toward the tomb. I followed more slowly because, by then, I was so tired and lost that I felt myself slipping back into the darkness. So, like a child who has lost its mother, I wanted to be near the place where I had seen him last, to cling to that which had given me life, even for a little while. I sat beside the empty tomb and let the tears come again. Blinded with them, my heart orphaned and aching sore, I peered again inside the tomb.

*(Her tone changes. She is seeing the light again.)*

I thought my tears had become stars and given me visions. Two brilliant lights hovered over the rolled linen. Yes, I did not tell you, the linen that Joseph had wound around the body was still in the same shape but with nothing in it. And the napkin that had been wound around his head was separated but not unwound. And the linens seemed to be guarded by white beings—they must have been angels . . .

And one of them, or both—I am not sure to this day—asked, "Woman, why are you weeping?" I wanted to say, why are you *not* weeping? Can you not tell that all the light has abandoned the earth? But I felt almost angry because they were full of light, and I resented them. So I turned away, but there was another man at the entrance.

The sun was rising and it lit up his hair, but I could not see his face—my eyes were blinded by light.

He too asked, "Why are you weeping?" By then I was feeling so sorry for myself that I said, "Oh please, if you are the gardener, tell me where you put my Lord, and I will take him away." I was really saying: I want to see him once more, to make sure that all that goodness really did happen. And then he called me by name. He called me by name!

The world had found its right place in the universe once again. The demons left, and the weight was lifted. The agony, the terrible sorrow of the last three days, was gone.

"Mariam," he called, and I fell on my knees. "Rabboni," I cried and bent to kiss his feet. But holiness stopped me. I couldn't quite touch him. I saw the stigmata on his feet and on his hands, and I was both joyful and bewildered. He said, "Don't cling to me now, I have not yet ascended to my Father, but I will soon. Go and tell my brothers that soon I will go to my Father and your Father, my God and your God."

And I understood. As always, I understood. First my heart, and then my mind. I had become, unto eternity, a witness to the resurrection. And I ran to tell them the good news.

## Questions to Ponder

1. Why do you suppose the legend arose that Mary Magdalene was a prostitute? Why was it important for the church to cast her in that role?

2. What demons does Mary mention? Is she talking about something unique to her, or are they the demons many women in today's society would encounter?

3. What is your own greatest demon that your faith in Jesus Christ has released you from?

4. What qualities of womanhood does Mary exemplify? Do you find them true in your own life? Obviously Mary of Magdala was one of the "liberated" women of the day. Yet she describes a quality common to women: "We knew what was expected of us, and we did it." How do you react to that?

FOUR

# The Dance in the Womb

## MOTHER TO ONE OF GOD'S CHOSEN

**Luke 1 (all of it); 3:19–20; 7:18–23**
**Matthew 3:1–12; 11:1–15; 14:3–12**
**Mark 6:17–29**

*(Elizabeth, the mother of John the Baptist, tells her story to the evangelist Luke.)*

*(As though in a dream)* The baby leapt and danced inside me at her approach. And I knew such joy that the memory of it has sustained me ever since. Through all the terrible loneliness of losing my son, I have remembered that joy and have been comforted.

Those were the days of miracles, awe, and laughter. Zechariah and I had given up all hope, but then he came home one day, angel-struck and dumb. Can you imagine Zechariah dumb, he whose tongue never stopped? Too bad you never met him, you would have liked his mind. Though, to tell you the truth, he was never the same after it happened.

*(She is recalled to the present.)* You look impatient. Yes, I should start at the beginning.

I was old, you see, by the time of the miracles. I had given up hoping, and the shame had become a part of me. I was barren. There is no greater shame to a Jewish woman. You know that, do you? Up here, on the hills of Judah, to be barren is to be despised. I keep wondering about this now that I am so old that only memories are alive. Everything else is dead. Why does the shame always fall on the woman? Well, well, it is no matter. *(She shrugs.)* It is too late for me to find out; your generation will know more, much more. Where was I? Ah yes.

So we had given up. Although every now and then, like Hannah with her Samuel, I still prayed for a son, but without Zechariah knowing. He'd call me a foolish old woman and laugh. He had his duties at the temple, you see. I was the one who was left alone, at home, without a baby to love and care for.

But that one wondrous day, when Zechariah returned home dumb, I had been praying secretly. And there he was, unable to speak. "What has happened to you?" I asked. He pointed to the skies, his eyes filled with a light I had never seen before. And then he brought his arm down and touched me on my belly, and then he made the motion of cradling and rocking. A part of me thought, that's it, he's lost his mind. The other part was not surprised.

He still smelled of incense and, through the open door, I saw that the people had followed him and kept staring at him. Something had happened at the temple. Zechariah was more powerful and yet more humble than ever before or since. So we put our arms around each other and laughed. I wanted to share in this wonderful, fearful thing that had come to pass.

And we loved each other, oh my soul. (*She laughs; Elizabeth is an earthy woman.*) It had been years, but a few weeks later I knew: My shame had been lifted. Well, lifted from my eyes at least, but I was embarrassed to be seen in public. For five months, I hid. I stayed home and sang and laughed to myself. Zechariah joined in the laughter whenever he was there. I planted seeds and waited for the flowers. I wove soft clothing and he made little toys for our son. Such peace-filled days. And then, when I had entered my sixth month, grace and joy came walking uphill in the shape of a lovely girl. I saw her in the distance, shaded my eyes from the hot Judean sun, and felt her floating toward me. Radiance walked with her, and I could tell—even though she was not showing—that she too was with child.

I had seen Mariam before, but it had been years, and I had forgotten how beautiful she was, what grace moved in her person. I walked toward her to ease the burden of a bundle on her head. I heard her voice, "Hail Elizabeth, peace be with you," and everything changed. My body became young, my spirit rose, and words came to my mouth and sang my joy. The baby danced in my womb. I was almost lifted from the ground. Where were the words coming from? I had nothing to do with them. "Blessed, blessed," I sang, "blessed are you among women and blessed is the fruit of your womb. How can I be so singled out that you, the mother of my Lord, have to come to see me?" I didn't stop to think, what am I saying? I knew that it was true, and she was not surprised. "You are blessed," I said, "because you believed in what the Lord promised to you. This is the fulfillment of all the promises made to humanity, you are carrying it." And instead of hugging her, I fell on my knees and touched her belly. The baby kept up his holy dancing in my body.

And Mariam, who had been so calm and smiling, now lifted her arms, threw back her head, and sang her song of joy. "My soul magnifies the Lord, and my spirit rejoices in God my Savior." And the song continued with echoes of Hannah, Sarah, and all the mothers that had gone before us. "He has put the mighty from their thrones and lifted up the lowly; he has filled the hungry with good things." (*Her voice has risen in a crescendo of joy. The memory is a gift that even death cannot take from her.*)

Ah, what days we spent together. Years later, when both our sons left us to turn the world upside down, I used to think how good it was that God let us have those happy months of waiting, of not knowing the sorrow that was to come. How good it was that we had time to think about promises fulfilled and not life snatched away. How good it is to anticipate joy while all around you the angels sing. (*She hears them still. She pauses and then continues her story.*)

Mariam stayed three months, until suddenly one day she said, "It is now time to face the world," and she returned to Joseph. Everything else slips from my mind now and then. But those three months remain the memory of perfect peace. We needed it, because what was to come was terror.

Soon after she left, my time came and the baby emerged, crying with a strong voice, his hair long and wild even then. On the day of the circumcision, when all the kinsmen and the neighbors wanted to call him Zechariah, I knew that his name would be "John." They thought I was a foolish, capricious woman until Zechariah asked for a tablet and wrote "John" on it with a white stone.

"What does this mean?" they asked, but suddenly Zechariah spoke. His wondrous words were music. I did not know that he had them in him. You understand now why I call these the days of miracles? "And you, child," he told his son, "you will be called the prophet of the Most High. For you will go before the Lord to prepare his way. That day," he prophesied, "will give light to those who sit in darkness, to guide our feet in the way of peace." Our guests did not suspect it, but we both knew that John would go before the son of Mary to prepare his way, and we were glad.

*(She moves closer to Luke and takes his hand into both of hers.)*

Years later, when Zechariah was gone and I, an old woman even then, asked for news of my son and heard that he was in Herod's dungeon, I wanted to beg the son of Mary to save my boy. But I knew that all that had happened, had happened as it was written. *(Resignedly)* You don't get the news of the coming of a child from an angel and expect to have a normal child like everyone else. You *wish* for it, but you know he is meant for something else: the *called* of God, the *chosen* of God. What a burden on those who give them birth. *(She bends her head and is silent.)*

Well, my young friend, the rest is history, isn't it? (*She pats Luke's hand and tries to comfort him.*) You have heard the gruesome story before. But first came his years of ministry in the wilderness. How strange our people are. John, who told them terrible things, and called them all kinds of hard names, was their favorite prophet. They loved him. They flocked to the desert to hear him and begged to be baptized. It hurt me to see him living all alone, animal skins barely covering his body, eating so little. I wondered how he stayed alive and looked so healthy. Of course, like any mother, I wanted him cleaned and dressed in softly woven *chitons*,[2] but I could not have that. So I comforted myself with his great popularity and his strength in telling the truth always, and unafraid.

When the other little boy who had grown up quietly came to the river to be baptized, John, the proud and unafraid, was so moved that he could not even bring himself to touch Jesus. John knew his days of preparation were coming to a close. The real thing had come. This was the day John had prepared for.

(*Back to a day of miracles. She loves recalling them.*)

What a wondrous day that was. I'm sure that you've heard all sorts of rumors, but I was there. I saw it. The skies did open up, and many of us did hear a voice; we knew that we were standing on holy ground. The awaited one had come. The voice crying in the wilderness had been right. John's time was over. The time of Jesus had come. And John accepted it with humility.

---

2. Long garments worn by men and even by women.

He turned his attention from the common people to Herod, and he, the weak and foolish king, had John arrested. For a while, Herod, afraid of the people—who knows, maybe even afraid of God—did not abuse John. He even let us visit him. On such a visit, when I thought *my* end was drawing near and I had gone to bid him peace, John looked at me with pain. "Remember the stories you told me, Mother?" he asked. "How I danced for joy in your body, when his mother came to you? That same joy came over me when he asked to be baptized. How sure I was then of who he was. But look at what is happening. Herod has not yet fallen, and the Romans still rule the land. Go ask him, is he the one, or are we to wait for another?" I felt such sorrow then. I thought, Has it all been for nothing? (*Her voice breaks.*)

I did not get my answer then, but later, when they killed Mariam's son, too. Then I had the answer. It was only that John had asked the wrong question. He should have asked, "Is this what the awaited one does? Choose to share all of humanity's sorrows? Choose suffering over passing happiness? Choose the cross over fame? Choose to obey God rather than man?" Of course John himself had made the choices that told him and us that he would rather obey God than man. And the awaited one, the Messiah, God's anointed, could do no less.

(*She drifts again into a beloved dream.*)

Oh, my child, my son, you did prepare the way, not only to life but also to death. What happened to that dance of joy that greeted your coming and his? It is still here in my heart. One day soon I will dance again with you.

## *Questions to Ponder*

1. Elizabeth does not express jealousy here toward Mary and her son, though she knows that her own son, John, comes to prepare the way for Jesus. How would you feel toward Mary's son if you were in Elizabeth's place?

2. What would it mean to have a child against all odds and then to lose him or her to a life of hardship for the sake of God's kingdom?

3. The friendship between Elizabeth and Mary must have been a strong one in order for Mary to leave her home and spend three months with Elizabeth while they were both pregnant. Why do you think they spent this time together? What does this biblical model of friendship say about the friendships between women?

4. On page 39 Elizabeth says, "The *chosen* of God. What a burden on those who give them birth." We do not hear in the Bible of Zechariah's or Joseph's sorrow at the death of their sons. Why do you suppose that is the case? What does the absence of these men's stories say about attitudes toward men and women in biblical days? Have those attitudes changed today?

# FIVE

# My Side of the Story
## WIFE TO ONE OF GOD'S CHOSEN

**Luke 4:38–39; 5:1–11**
**Matthew 4:18–22**
**Mark 1:16–20, 29–31; 14:66–72**
**John 1:35–51; 21:1–19**

*Even a cursory knowledge of the Gospels reveals that we know nothing about Peter's wife, and most of what she says below is based on the imagination, except for the passages about Peter. She is not a mythical character, however. If Peter had a mother-in-law, as mentioned in the above passages, he had to have a wife. Who was she? What did she think about her husband's leaving her to follow Jesus?*

*(Peter's wife speaks to a congregation of early converts.)*

I want to tell you my side of the story now. Will you listen? Have you even heard about me? Do you know *my* name? No. I am the nameless wife.

He started dropping by the house—his new friend Jesus—before Simon thought anything about leaving us and going with him. I call him Simon. That's who he was when I met him, and that's who he remained for me until . . . Well, I'll tell you that when the time comes. I like to take things in order. If my life was not as well ordered as it is, I would not have survived.

Simon was hooked, like one of his own fish, I told him. Jesus would come in, and a hush would fall on Simon. This was strange. You see, Simon was a big talker. Yes, he was! Always ready to express an opinion, full of all kinds of enthusiasm. If he met somebody he liked, he would tell the person that right away. And if he didn't like you, he'd tell you that to your face in a minute. I was used to him. I knew him well. Or so I thought.

Our parents had arranged for us to marry each other when we were children. But when he saw me as a girl in full bloom, he came up to me and said, "You will be my wife. I am glad you will be my wife, because I like you. I like what I see. And it's a good thing. Because, you know, I wouldn't go through with it if I didn't like you."

I didn't know what to say. I blushed and lowered my eyes, but he took me by the hand and pulled me to my house and announced to my mother and father: "She will be my wife and I will be good to her." Just like that. That was Simon for you. Impetuous always.

(*This is a woman very comfortable in her relationship with the male friends of her husband. She is not shy, and she knows who she is.*)

James and John, the Zebedee boys, the sons of thunder, were in and out of the house every day. The three of them and Andrew, too, Simon's brother, were inseparable. As different from one another they were as night and day, but you could tell they liked each other and that was good. I was never lonely those days. Those boys were coming and going. I enjoyed baking for them and feeding them, and they talked together about everything under the sun.

In the twilight they went out to the lake to fish and returned with much noise in the morning. My mother made the fire, and I cleaned the fish and then cooked them. The place smelled delicious. Simon would sleep for a few hours and then the boys would come by and it would start all over again. Things were good. I didn't want them to change. I worried a bit about what would happen if the other boys married. Would I like their wives? Would we continue our close fellowship and rejoice in each other's company? But we were young and thought life would never change.

(*Her tone changes. There is still some ambivalence at the memory.*)

Then *he* came walking in one day. "Peace be with you, little children," he said. That affectionate word we have in our language. No, it doesn't mean "little" children. It means dear friends. A nice expression. I don't know how else to explain it. Loving-like. You understand. Well, the moment I saw him and heard his voice I knew that nothing would ever be the same again. Simon? He hadn't a clue. He was fascinated.

Simon and the other boys didn't go to the synagogue much. They were reverent, respectful boys, but they didn't go in for all that religious stuff the Pharisees liked so much. But when he walked in, Simon got all quiet and listened. 'Cause Jesus always talked about his Father and the

kingdom of God, and Simon didn't think that was anything like Pharisee-talk. He thought it was the best news
he had ever heard. He never put the two together. God-talk
from Jesus didn't bother him like it did from everybody
else. So I knew we were in trouble.

Whenever he came by, Simon dropped his nets and
fish, whistled to James, John, and Andrew, and the four of
them listened and watched Jesus as he walked about
Capernaum, with hordes of people always following
behind him. I started getting very worried. One day my
mother woke up and couldn't get out of bed. She was
burning with fever. I was really frightened. I dipped a
cloth in cold water and kept putting it on her forehead.
Simon had come in from fishing and had gone straight to
sleep. I sat there weeping a bit. My mother had never
been sick before and I was so worried. And then, suddenly, I heard the noise of the crowd and Jesus walked in.
He came in by himself and, just from the way he entered,
I knew none of the others would dare follow him. There
was that quiet that surrounded him; like an arm that held
him up, it wouldn't let him fall. He scared me a little bit.
I couldn't be indifferent to him. I couldn't feel with him
the way I felt when I was with John and James. I kept
thinking I had to make promises to him, and I resented
that. It was as if his presence demanded your whole
attention even before he opened his mouth.

I ran to the back and called Simon. "Please wake up,
Simon. Your friend is here and my mother is very sick."
Simon woke up immediately and together we came to the
front room. I didn't see Jesus at first. He had walked to the
corner where my mother's bed was and stood looking

down at her. Simon, being Simon, went right up to him and asked, "Can you do anything for her?"

(*Her eyes are filled with the pictures of that day. She can see everything as it happened on that particular morning.*)

The people outside had started creeping in. He didn't look at any of them. He was looking at Simon with those eyes that said, your question is the most important in the world. Jesus was standing behind my mother's head. He put his hand on her forehead and was still. Then he moved to the side of the bed, facing her, and took her by the hand. He said something—to this day I don't know what—and my mother sat up and smiled at him. Before I could protest, she was up and around, getting the fish cleaned and ready for broiling. It's a good thing too, because the house started filling up with the sick. I could never have managed by myself. And though I was so happy for my mother, and for myself, too, I was filled with foreboding. Nothing was going to be the same for us after this. Jesus hardly ate. Neighbors and people I had never seen kept bringing in their sick, and he spoke to some, touched others, and prayed over a few of them until Simon finally put a stop to it because Jesus looked exhausted.

A couple of days later, what I had feared happened. (*She is now telling a story that has become familiar, but only she knows the details.*) The boys had gone fishing. They all told me the story later, breathless from excitement, loaded down as they were with hundreds of fish. All night long they had moved the boat and cast the nets only to pull them up empty. Downcast, they stood around, knee deep in the water, washing the nets, doing some mending, hesitant to come home empty-handed.

Then they saw the new prophet, the healer, Jesus. He was walking toward the shore, followed by hundreds of people from all around Capernaum. The boys watched to see what would happen next. They looked at each other and wondered. "Should we go rescue him? They are pressing very close to him." Then Jesus stood for a few minutes looking at them in the sea and saw that they had caught nothing.

He waded straight up to Simon, smiled at him, and climbed into his boat. Simon stopped what he was doing and rushed to him. "Simon," Jesus said, "take me a bit far from the shore so I can see all the people at the same time. I don't want them falling in the water. Let me sit in the boat and talk to them." Simon climbed in immediately and rowed with all his strength. "That's good," Jesus said and he turned to the crowd. As was his habit he started telling them about the Scriptures, about his Father, and about God's kingdom. And again he said what had become a refrain for him, one that made chills run up and down my spine. "Today this Scripture has been fulfilled in your sight." The people were very quiet. They listened. And then he lifted up his arms and blessed them, and they moved away from the shore.

Simon stood there gaping. Jesus again turned to him and said, "Come Simon, let us go to deeper waters, and there cast your nets." Simon told me he laughed. "I thought, here is a carpenter from landlocked Nazareth. He knows nothing about fishing."

"'Master,' Simon told him, 'look at our nets. John and James and I have been fishing all night. Nothing. We caught nothing.' He kept looking at me," Simon recalled, "with those deep eyes that saw through me. So I agreed. 'I will do it, though, since you are asking it.' So I rowed, Jesus helping me, and when he said, 'Here,' I stopped and cast the nets as far as I could. Before I let go, I felt them sink. A multitude of fish ran to them. You'd think they had been waiting for me. I pulled, Jesus helped, and we couldn't lift them. Jesus had kept his eyes on the other two, James and John, and motioned with his arm for them to come here. They rowed as fast as they could and, with mouths open, started pulling with us. The boats filled with fish and I was filled with fear."

Simon couldn't tell me the rest. It was John who did. He told me how Simon, trembling, fell and asked Jesus to leave him. "I am a sinful man," he said. *Typical Simon,* I thought. But I knew everything had changed. John, who can be exasperating and sweet beyond words, told me the rest. "Jesus pulled Simon up and said, 'Do not be afraid.' And then he said to the rest of us, 'Let's take the fish to the market, boys.' And as we rowed those heavy boats to the shore, he looked at us," John continued, "and laughed. 'Come,' he told us, 'from now on you will be fishing, and your nets will be pulling people in.'"

When I heard this, I asked Simon, "What does he mean? What does he mean?" Simon answered, "I don't know. All I know is that I will follow him to the ends of the earth."

*(With a sad smile but with the resignation of Middle Eastern women.)*

He wasn't even sad when he told me. After selling the boat and the catch, he gave me more money than I had ever seen, kissed me and my mother good-bye, and, arm in arm with John and James, went to get Andrew. Then they all left with Jesus. *(With the practicality of a woman who can't be fooled.)* It didn't do any good to cry. I knew I had lost him, but I also knew that they would all be back to clean up, to eat, to spend a day or two resting. Where else could they go?

During those three years, Simon was happier and more content than I had ever seen him. He was triumphant at times; he was hard-headed and proud; he made his mistakes (he would not have been Simon had he not done that); and, finally, he almost died from grief. He was, after all, Simon, full of love and faithfulness and cowardice and fear. I'm sure you've heard how he denied his best friend in the end. The whole world knows his shame. I had heard of the arrest and rushed to Jerusalem, and I was there when the cock crowed in the morning. I saw Simon put his head in his hands and heard him weep bitterly. His heart was broken. It was the saddest moment of his life. "How could I deny him?" he asked me again and again, and all I could think of was, the same way you denied me, but I didn't say it.

Then something happened, and that is when I started calling him Petros also. After the resurrection . . . *(She defies the whole world here.)* Yes, don't look surprised, I saw him dead and I saw him alive afterward, so I know what I am talking about. But even if I had not seen him, the change in Simon would have made me a believer. The story I told you at the beginning, about our cooking fish by the shore, that same scene happened again just for Simon. And here by this lake Jesus cooked for him and asked him, "Petros, do you love me?"

Mind you, Simon told me all this. "'Petros, do you love me?' He asked me that three times," Simon said. Every time Simon remembered, his eyes filled with tears. "Petros, do you love me?"

It was after that that Petros changed. (*She too has come to a conclusion; she is no longer ambivalent.*) I never saw him afraid again. He started reminding me of Jesus. The same quiet strength enveloped him. Between his travels and his preaching he came home to see me, to be with me for a day or two. He was serious and full of wisdom, but every now and then I missed the boy Simon—his moods and enthusiasms, his fears and his ups and downs.

I knew the end would not be easy for him, any more than it had been for his master and best friend. Was it worth it? you ask me. Everybody asks me. How can a poor woman like me judge that? He cast his nets, and they were filled. He cast his life, and it was filled. Some say he lost it. Petros said he found it.

And he never looked back. Why should I?

## Questions to Ponder

1. At the beginning of this monologue Peter's wife comes across as angry, as someone whose side of the story has been ignored. By the end of the monologue she says she does not need to look back, implying that she has no regrets. What do you think changed her perspective?

2. It is easy to forget the power of telling our stories and hearing the stories of others. Peter's wife clearly needs to tell her own story here. When, in your own life, has

the power of telling your own story or hearing someone else's story been important? What are the stories
that we, as individuals or as a nation, do not listen to
carefully?

3. Peter's wife pays a high price for Peter's decision to follow Christ. Have you ever made a decision to follow
Christ? What was the cost to you? Was it worth it?

4. There was a time when we admired the courage of
missionaries. There are far fewer of them in the
church today, but those who do this work can place
great demands on their families. Perhaps that is why
so many of the early church workers chose not to
marry. Has this changed for those who risk all for the
gospel today? Is it easier to follow Christ as a single
person than as one who is married?

# Even the Dogs Eat the Crumbs

## THE FAITH OF AN OUTCAST

**Mark 7:24–30**
**Matthew 15:21–28**

*(The Syrophoenician woman tells her story to anyone who will listen.)*

Oh, I can't run fast enough to her. To see her again, no longer racked by terror, but peaceful, as I remember the beloved face, without the contortions . . . To see my daughter whole again, that's what I live for.

Everyone can hear my songs and loud tears of joy. From deep within I am shouting my thanks to the God of life. I do not doubt that she will be well when I reach home—not for a moment do I doubt him. Him. The man of love, the man of strength, the man of life.

*(She is talking to the curious who are following her home after her encounter with Jesus.)*

The rumors had reached us even here in the city of Tyre. This miracle man, the young Nazarene, was turning the world upside down wherever he went. How people talked of him! Many with love, others with hate and envy.

From the rumors, I knew that he was the one I was waiting for, and I set out to find him. "Tell me, tell me what you know," I had begged all my friends. "Tell me the moment you hear that he is coming anywhere near."

The Jews don't like us so near their northern borders. From time immemorial our people have fought each other. But the merchants still come and go and Tyre-by-the-Sea is an important city, fabled from before the time of Alexander. With merchants and sailors came the news of the Galilean. The Greek language of my father helped me to talk to most foreigners, to beg them to tell me if there was any cure for my beautiful, my darling little daughter.

What a lovely child she had been in infancy. Her smile lit up the home and joy filled us. Then, suddenly, screams started in the night; her beloved face was twisted with a terror unknown to me, and my days were turned to darkness. "The demon has possessed her," all our local doctors said. They warned me not to have any hope. Her father talked of killing her and me. But I had tasted life, I knew it was good, and I was determined to love my child back to health.

And then I heard of the Galilean preaching down there by the Sea of Galilee. The messengers told us that he could not get away from the sick. People were bringing the sick to him by the thousands. Even touching his garment healed them.

(She pauses for just a minute and addresses her followers.)

I knew who he was. I had heard the ancient scribes read to me, and I knew how the Jews had waited all these many years for the Son of David. I had longed for such a coming myself. Because this God I had heard about answered the fervent longings of his people, I longed for him. What he demanded of them was obedience. That I understood, and that I could give. He was a God who kept his promises, and this child of mine was a promise. I knew how to respect an honest agreement.

Jesus finally slipped away across the border and came to rest in Tyre. They tried to hide his coming. They were walking through the town, he and a group of his followers, heading toward the sea. The people of the town hadn't heard the news yet. (*She confronts the curious once more.*) You may think it was chance that made them pass by my house, but I looked out the door and there he was. And I knew it was my fervent longing that brought him near me. I ran out of the house as I was.

I ran. "Son of David," I called, "Son of David." He kept on walking and some of his followers tried to stop him. He turned and looked at me for just a second, and there was such a terrible weariness on his face that I almost lost my nerve. He looked as though all energy had been drained from him and he was barely standing up. His friends pushed me back, but I followed, my eyes never losing sight of him. I felt that if I lost him, I might as well give up and die. They stopped by the sea, searching for a boat, I think, and I pushed ahead and fell on my knees.

"Look at her," his friends mocked. "She is like a dog. Look at the foreigner begging. Send her away," they said to him, "she is a nuisance." He had been looking out to sea, as though he longed to leave all of us and be alone. He said—it was like he was talking to himself, but I heard him clearly—"I was sent only to the lost sheep of the house of Israel."

(*She pauses now and turns to face them.*) There is this thing about the Jews, you see. They make you feel that only they know God, that nobody else does. But he didn't make me feel left out. It was almost like a question that he was examining in his mind. The lost sheep of the house of Israel . . . It didn't matter to me. I would join any lost tribe, if he would just look at me again. "Lord, help me," I said, "have mercy. My daughter, my baby, has been taken over by a demon."

Again he was very quiet, looking out to the sea, the taunts of his friends in his ears. "Lord, help me," I cried again, sure that his face revealed nothing but compassion. "Lord, have mercy on me."

Finally he turned his head and looked at his followers. "It is not fair to take the children's bread and throw it to the dogs," he said to them, not to me, and they laughed, agreeing. But his eyes were very serious, looking at them, searching them, as though he had forgotten all about me.

But I knew about dogs and about children. I knew about Jews and Canaanites and Greeks. And I knew that only *he* could heal my daughter. I did not budge. "Yes, Lord," I agreed, "Yet even the dogs eat the crumbs that fall from their master's table."

He looked at me full in the eyes then, surprise in his own eyes and then relief; almost—I am embarrassed to think this—almost admiration I saw in them. I knew what the answer would be. He had read a heart that longed for nothing but the healing of a child.

"O woman," he said, and there was surprise in his voice, "your faith is great!" (*Full of gratitude, she weeps aloud.*) He knew. He knew that for me he was the awaited one, the Jewish Messiah, God's Son, God's promise. Great love and power reached me like a surge of energy. Suddenly he looked radiant, no longer tired.

"Let it be as you desire," he said. "Your daughter is well." Not your daughter *will be* well, but your daughter *is* well. Oh, words of comfort unspeakable. Your daughter is well. And I had never doubted that he would do it.

*(She runs into the house. She points to her daughter.)*

And now here is my darling, her beautiful face as peaceful as God created it, asleep on her bed. She opens her eyes and looks at me and smiles. The demon is gone. *(She lifts the child up. Her face is radiant.)* The God of love has my undying devotion. I will praise his name for ever and ever.

## Questions to Ponder

1. How does this telling of the story of the Syrophoenician woman differ from your own previous understanding of this story?

2. How do you feel about Jesus discovering something important about his ministry from a woman who is considered an outcast? What do we have to learn from those who are outcasts today?

3. Place yourself into the middle of this story. Would you be the sick daughter, the distraught mother, Jesus, or one of the crowd following Jesus, or some other character? How would you tell the story from that person's perspective?

# Spending It All for the Saints

## THE FIRST CONVERT IN THE LAND
## OF ALEXANDER

**Acts of the Apostles 16:11–40**

*(Lydia reminisces with Luke.)*

Oh Luke, to tell you this story would be to repeat what you saw with your own eyes, eh? What is that? You want a woman's interpretation of the events? How like you, my dear friend. I am so happy to see you again, beloved physician. Do I remember those first days, the days of miracles and light? How could I ever forget! How could I ever forget a minute of those days?

*(She pauses and peers at Luke. She realizes she will not see him again.)*

Now the time has come for me to follow in the footsteps of our beloved Paul. Though the privilege of suffering for the sake of the holy name has not been given to me as it was to him. But the end is coming near, and I spend my final hours thinking about every scene of those blessed days when I first saw the light.

*(She smiles, a proud old woman remembering her youth.)*

Do you remember what I was? A Greek woman with Roman citizenship, a business woman known for my success in weaving and dying the marvelous purple cloth that the nobles love to wear. I laugh to think of it now, that something that caused Paul to lift the eyebrow became the source of so much help to him and to the church. *(She chuckles.)* I dealt with the rich of Philippi, you see, since all the important citizens of the Roman colony came to me for their chitons, togas,[3] and fancy dress. Paul was ambivalent about the rich. He knew how to use them since he had been close to nobility himself. He knew the value of Roman citizenship and, when the situation called for it, claimed it without hesitation. But at the same time, he who knew how to work very hard—remember how calloused his hands were?—had some veiled contempt for those who did not use their money for the brethren.

*(A pause. The memory is vivid. Her eyes see it as it is happening.)*

Ach, those days. We were by the river that one blessed, unforgettable day. Dappled shadows played with the light on the glistening water. The trees—bitter-smelling daphne, aromatic figs and silver olives—bent to kiss the waters. I was there on my knees, checking on the work of the girls, as they washed the purple dyed wool. I remember how the color changed in the water, deep blue and indigo, like Homer's wine-red sea, and the stream of purple running swiftly downhill with the water. The picture

---

3. Chitons were the inner long garments worn by both men and women, and togas were the shorter, outer loose robes.

has stayed with me of that moment when I heard his voice. He boomed it aloud: "Good women, is there a place for prayer nearby?" Without getting up, I turned my head and saw you all walking toward us on the water's edge. I remember seeing *you*, so young and golden in the light, with one of your feet in the water, the other on the shore. You looked like you were dancing. I saw Paul and Silas, in their worn-out chitons and tunics, looking sort of rough, very Jewish, I thought. I wondered what Jewish men were doing walking on the Sabbath. "We are looking for a place of worship, of prayer," Silas said in that sweet, deferential voice of his.

I stood up then. Something told me these were not ordinary travelers. I couldn't take my eyes off Paul's face. I was riveted. I was a very courageous woman. Do you remember? I was used to dealing with men because they were the ones who bought my products, but I found myself trembling. All of you came and stood nearby waiting, not saying anything. Where did my words come from? I said to Paul: "Here is some cool water for you and your friends to drink, but I don't know of a synagogue nearby. Would you pray with us?"

*(She bends her head, deeply moved by the memory of the moment that changed her life.)*

He didn't say, "What do you think? We are not Greeks to mingle with women at our prayers. We are Jews." No, he looked at me and said, "Tell me to whom you pray, noble lady." And I said, "To the Lord God, I worship the Lord God." And I looked at him as though he held the secret of this god I worshiped. I wondered for a moment, will he cast doubt on this god I mentioned? But he said very kindly. "Yes, would you like to bring all your women here, near this tree, and let us pray together?" I dropped the wet cloth I was holding then. I didn't even care about the expense, the hours upon hours of work. "Come, girls," I called, "come, all of you."

They crept toward me shyly, keeping as far from the men as possible, but when they saw all of you kneeling, they looked at me, questioning. What was the proper thing to do? I dropped to my knees and they did the same. They all lowered their eyes, but I couldn't. I had to keep looking at that short, dark Jew who mesmerized me with his eyes. And then he started talking to Jesus. It was like a conversation between friends, very quiet, and we could hear only his side, but there was no question that there was someone there listening to him and answering him. And then he looked at us, smiled, and said, "I'll tell you the most important news of your life."

*(She starts softly, her voice rising gradually as she reaches the central truth of her life.)*

And he told us about the man Jesus, about his death and resurrection, and about his own life-changing encounter on the road to Damascus. I knew then that I had found the one I had been looking for. All I had worshiped, all the prayers I had uttered in my lifelong longing for God, all the best I had heard of Greek philosophy, all the hints I had received from nature and the myths, everything came together and made sense. Everything had been a preparation for this one central truth of God becoming man. Oh, the harmony of that knowledge. Oh, the sweet satisfaction of knowing that we were not alone.

And then the peace, when he baptized me and the girls in the name of the Lord Jesus.

*(The following are the memories of a woman who experienced life fully.)*

Remember what I did then? I see you smiling. I ran home and you all came later, guided by my girls. I prepared the greatest feast of my life. Everything that was good and rich in our lovely part of the world was readied for you. How good the fish tasted that day and how delicious it smelled as it sizzled on the fire. I can still taste the lemon on its white succulent flesh, the warm figs and the cool wine. Everything became significant. Every moment was imbued with light. I sensed God's hand in all creation. I felt the love of the Lord Jesus in every good gift. And how you all sang. I was then very thankful for all the money I had made because I knew I would spend it to make Paul's and Silas' lives easier.

When they said good-bye and all of you went back into the city, I was uneasy. Would that silly girl that had followed you, crying out in her eerie voice, cause you trouble? I have thought a great deal about her since then, that poor slave girl that the horrid men took advantage of. She had a gift that they forced her to use as a curse—the gift of seeing beyond what the eye sees. When Paul ordered the demon out of her and she was healed, she then became useless to the men. I have wondered many times since then what happened to her. When Paul released her, was he helping or hurting her? These are hard questions that confront us now. Someday, I would like to know the answers. But those days, when I heard about the arrest of the two saints, the beatings and the blood, I was so angry!

A whole crowd of us came into the city then and camped outside the prison. I could imagine Paul and Silas in those stocks, their poor bleeding feet wide apart, the agony of pain on the legs, and they? They were singing! That sound, drifting over the marble and the stones in the night, has been with me whenever life has seemed too sad to bear. The manly voices starting softly, broken at first from the pain that pulled the sore muscles, getting stronger and stronger as the spirit filled them and strengthened them. Ah, what a memory that is!

*(She pauses and listens to the sounds inside her head. Then she is reminded of Luke's presence.)*

By the way, I don't know what happened to the rest of you. Did they keep you hidden somewhere, so that you would not meet with the same fate? I see you nodding. No, don't be ashamed after all these years. All of us who suffered for the faith did our best to protect as many of the brothers and sisters as was possible. Paul always told us that the struggle had to continue no matter how many of us were imprisoned.

The atmosphere was suddenly very heavy that night. No wind blew. A rumble started. I was not aware of what was coming because all I could think of was the suffering within. And then the whole earth seemed to shake. The stones moved and started tumbling. Our group was out in the open already, so we simply waited for the shaking to stop. There was not much else we could do except pray and wait on the Lord.

From a house nearby the jailer ran out wailing. I saw him in the courtyard as a flash of light rent the sky. He pulled a sword, drew his arm back, and seemed ready to do away with himself. One of the Romans' less attractive customs, I must add. Immediately, out of the dark, the depths of that prison, Paul's voice resounded: "Do not harm yourself. We are all here." And then it struck me. Why hadn't the prisoners escaped? Was the singing of these bound and bleeding men such a miracle that the others could not even move?

*(She has told this story many times before. She is like a Greek actress, imitating voices, assuming roles in the telling.)*

The jailer started calling to his servants. "Torches, I need torches!" Ten of them ran with lights. We followed. In the depths, under falling stones, Paul and Silas sat. Their bonds had been loosened, the ugly stocks had split in two, and still they sat and smiled up at us.

When I ran to them, Paul said, "No, Lydia, my sister, it is his turn." And so it was. The jailer had them lifted and carried to his house. He himself washed their wounds and poured oil on them. He gave them clean clothes to wear, and all the while the man wept. He couldn't do enough for them. After they had eaten, he fell on his knees before them. "Tell me, please, what can I do to be saved?" I remember thinking at that moment, why is it that all of us ask that question of Paul? What is it about him that makes us think that he holds a key to our salvation?

"Do?" Paul answered him. "You don't have to *do* anything, my friend." But, of course, the whole time the man was *doing*, acting as a servant toward them. "You don't have to do anything," Paul repeated, "but you must *believe* in the Lord Jesus Christ."

They all sat down then and waited. There were so many people there. The man's wife and children, all his servants, and as many of the guards as could fit. The prisoners were standing out in the yard. No one had escaped, which I still remember as one of the strangest events of those eventful days. And Paul started on his favorite story. Talking about the Lord Jesus changed his face somehow. Awe and familiarity combined. A kind of longing that never ended. A sharing of what was most precious to him. He was talking about someone he knew, someone he had seen and longed for with a nostalgia known only to him. And most of all, he spoke of him with love and assurance.

*(Matter-of-factly. She has thought about this many times.)*

You see, I have this theory about Paul. I think everyone who heard him talk about Jesus believed him. They may not have wanted to believe, and they turned away, but I don't think there was a single listener who did not believe that Paul was talking about the Son of God. What made us different from those who turned away was this: Some of us wanted to follow this Jesus. Others did not want anything to do with someone who made demands on their lives. So that is where we parted. But I never doubted that they all believed.

Does that make sense to you? Yes, I see you agree. So we had a huge celebration that night in the midst of the debris from the earthquake. And a baptism of everyone in the jailer's company. It was morning by then. That was when Paul showed his other side, the one that said, I will be humbled for the sake of the Lord, but ignorant and mean people will not take advantage of us without an explanation. We have our dignity, and that must not be violated.

We were guests of the happy jailer. He wanted to serve all of us because we were associated with these two saints he had in his home. And then the officers of the city came running. "Let these men go," they told the jailer. "You may go in peace," the host said to the two injured men. "They said you are free to go." But Paul looked at Silas and then at the jailer. "Go back to them and say we will not go quietly. Tell them that we are Roman citizens. Tell them that we were not tried before any authorities. We were grabbed by a mob, and the magistrates were the ones who gave the orders to beat us like common thieves. They did it publicly and now they want to get out of this in secret? No. Let them come themselves and release us publicly."

And so it was. The magistrates were scared. The fame of the two extraordinary men had reached them, and they were frightened. Of course, what scared them the most was that Paul had Roman citizenship. They did not know that the one citizenship that mattered was the kingdom of heaven. But as I said, Paul wanted it known that they were not dealing with religious charlatans or magicians. He wanted it known that they were intelligent and respectable men who had the news of the Lord Jesus Christ to impart.

So the magistrates came and apologized publicly, and we stood there listening and smiling our thanks. But they were so frightened of these men who were turning the world upside down that they said, "Please leave the city." So we all went to my house, where they stayed

until all their wounds were healed. By that time we had
an ekklesia[4] formed and worshiped every day. My house,
large as it was, filled with the sisters and brothers. It was
a time of joy.

*(She pauses. Up to this point she has been telling a story
shared by both of them. Now she tells him something new.)*
And then all of you left for Thessaloniki. From then
on, we lived for Paul's letters. I never stopped thanking
God that I was chosen to be the first in Greece to hear the
Word, and I never stopped being thankful for the hospitality I was able to offer.

*(She listens to Luke's question.)* Well, yes, Luke, I did
spend all I made for the saints. That is why I was given
such a rich trade. There were so many needs among the
faithful here in Philippi and elsewhere. It doesn't matter
that not much is left. I took care of my household and the
household of faith, and the Lord has never let us go hungry. The memory of those early days sustained me. And
the news from Paul and all the brothers and sisters filled
us with joy.

We all felt that we were Paul's children in God. And
maybe it will be forgiven me if I say that he always had a
very tender love for us in Philippi. I think his last hours
must have been less painful because he felt our prayers.
But soon I will know. No need for tears, Luke. I see you
now and remember that golden young man walking by
the edge of the river, like a dancer. How eager you were,
how full of curiosity. And you have not lost the longing to

---

4. The "calling out" of people into a congregation. The Greek word for
church.

know all that there is to know about the brethren. How
your love has sustained us. Peace be with you, my friend.
Until we meet again.

## Questions to Ponder

1. St. Paul has often been called a misogynist—someone
   who dislikes women. After reading this story from
   Acts, where so many women are named, what do you
   think of that description?

2. Christians are called to be humble and sacrificial,
   something that Paul obviously knew about. But, as
   this monologue points out, he is not afraid to confront
   the authorities either. How can we use this story in
   our own struggle on behalf of the poor, the helpless,
   and the needy?

3. Lydia is unusual in that she is a business woman
   working with men in the marketplace. She seems to
   break all the ancient rules about subservient and quiet
   women. What qualities do you see in Lydia that are
   worth emulating?

4. Lydia was a successful business woman, yet she gave
   away everything she had and trusted that God would
   provide for her. How does that example challenge you?

# Jealous of God's Favor
## MIRIAM'S SECRET

**Exodus 2:1–10, 21–22; 15:20–21**
**Numbers 12 (all of it)**

*(Miriam considers her exile.)*

I stood there hidden in the reeds and saw it happening.
Exactly as I had seen it in the dream, when the baby was
still in Mother's womb. Exactly. And I was not surprised.

The basket floated well. For a moment, panic gripped
me that it would sink, that our clever sealing with the tar
hadn't set. But then I remembered the dream, and panic
left me. Yahweh is a trustworthy God. *(She remembers the
scene vividly.)*

I heard the princess and her women arriving with
laughter and laundry. She did not hold herself aloof from
them but joked with the slave girls. I peeked through the
reeds gently, quietly, saw the laughing face, and knew
again that I had chosen the right princess, for Pharaoh
had other daughters. But this was the face that came to
me in the dream. First it was our mother's face in the con-

tortions of giving birth—a face of pain—replaced gradually by this darker, younger face of the Egyptian princess. And as the baby wailed, I saw her lit by love and pity, and I knew she would protect him. I knew it as I know the cruel fact of my exile this minute.

I gave the basket a push. It glided swiftly toward the laundry of the princess and was caught by the linen they had spread on the reeds. The squeals of the girls discovering something unexpected came to my ears. I waited. I wanted her to see him first. I knew the moment they opened the basket, because a hush fell over them. I could not see them, but I sensed what was happening. He was such a beautiful baby. His face was open with a perpetual smile, but in the darkness of his prison he had been crying. She fell in love with him immediately, wanting to protect him, and by the time I appeared through the reeds I knew that she would want to keep him. *(This is a woman who learned to plan and lead early in life.)*

For throughout the months of my mother's confinement, I had visited the banks of the river, trying to learn the habits of the women who came there. I loved the water—the sounds of the Nile, the sudden green that sprang on its banks after the floods, the feel of the wet earth along the flowing movement—and I knew who came there regularly; I had spotted her from afar many a time. Then, after the dream, I let her see me occasionally, so that by the time she found the basket, she would not be surprised to see me appear on the bank. It was almost as though we were friends. Our eyes would meet, and she would smile.

So on that day, I appeared in my quiet way and looked at the baby, together with the dumbfounded girls. They must have thought he was a god and feared to touch him. But I bowed to her and then tickled his chin as I had always done at home, and he laughed. I saw a thrill go through her at the sound.

The princess looked at me, a worry line between her brows. "It is a Hebrew boy, isn't it?" she asked unnecessarily. I nodded. We both knew what happened to Hebrew boys. "You need a nurse, Your Highness," I volunteered. "Shall I find you a good Hebrew woman to nurse him?" Great relief smoothed her face. "Yes, what a clever girl you are!" More than you know, I thought, more than you know. And I ran.

Mother was waiting where I had left her, tears still in her eyes from letting him go. I gave her my hand. "Come," I said, and she wiped her tears. We ran until we came close to the royal laundry, and then I slowed down purposefully and Mother followed my example. The reclaiming of a son became a business transaction. They were both pretending. "I will pay you wages to nurse him," the lovely princess said, and we almost burst out laughing. My mother held her favorite again, her precious baby boy, and I rejoiced to see her face smiling as she put him to her bosom. And I felt the quiet joy and assurance that what had been revealed to me in the dream held true. He was a trustworthy God. (*With conviction*) He is a trustworthy God.

(*With dismay*) But look at me now. My skin, burned and wrinkled from the desert sun, is white with leprosy.

Can it be? (*She looks at her hands. Pauses.*) I know now
why it happened. No, I did not understand it at the
moment I complained with Aaron against Moses. I had
been angry with my baby brother many a time before and
had expressed my anger. And nothing happened to me
then. Moses and Aaron have both listened to me on many
occasions. Moses, like me, of course, listens to another's
voice. I see it in his eyes. He seems to be looking at us, but
inside he is listening to the Lord. Almost always, I have
understood this, but Aaron, poor Aaron, he will listen to
anybody and be swayed, even by the motley crew the
three of us led out of Egypt. How many years has it been?

Moses and I have understood each other. From the
time I put him back to our mother's breast we have
understood each other. All the years she nursed him I
talked to him; I told him stories of our Hebrew people
and never let him forget who he is.

But Moses, now that he is old and tired, does forget
things. He forgets duties and responsibilities to those
closest to him. Poor old Aaron, he can't help being a fool
at times, but must Moses ignore him? And how dare he
marry this young Cushite woman? It is this that angered
Aaron and me. Moses, the meekest of men, forgetting
Zipporah, the wife who lived through all the miseries
with him . . . Without a thought he put her away; she,
who suffered for him, becomes a thing to be tossed aside,
and he succumbs to the charms of a foreigner.

(*With the passion of a visionary*) He should never have
married anyone. That kind of divided loyalty hurts people like us. Our visions should be enough. We can't

serve two masters. That is why no man has ever claimed my loyalty.

*(She is recalled to the present.)*

But immediately after my protest against Moses, leprosy claimed my skin. Now I keep thinking of death and of my parents. I must not forget what happened in the desert. I must tell the story. I remember my father and his pride in me, even though I was a girl.

*(As if addressing her mother)* Poor dear, if you had only lived. The son you thought would never survive to learn the Hebrew story has become the prophet who *makes* the story. What years these have been. Full of misery and hardship, yet full of glory . . . *(with memories of triumph)* leading a fickle people out of Egypt, the three of us, your children Miriam, Aaron, and Moses. *(She is lost in her memories; then a revelation dawns.)*

Where was I? Ah, the awful moment. It struck me, this miserable jealousy, this terrible thing that blinded me even to my love of Moses when the Lord spoke in that frightening pillar of cloud. He said of Moses, "With him I speak mouth to mouth clearly, and not in dark speech . . . and he beholds the form of the Lord." Ah, it struck me then, "Why not me, oh Lord? Why have you come to me only in dreams, never mouth to mouth?" And I felt it then, this sickness on the skin.

*(She looks at her hands. Disgust turns to surprise, to revelation.)* Sickness of the skin? No, rather, it was the sickness in my soul, my terrible jealousy of God's favor. That is what made me sick. *(Looks at her arms and touches her face.)*

Ah, Lord, I remember that moment when the ecstasy came upon me, there by the sea, when the enemy was vanquished at last and we were free. How sweet it was to find your words on my tongue. "Sing, sing to the Lord for he has triumphed gloriously. The horse and his rider he has thrown to the sea." (*She pauses, remembering; sings the verse this time as though in a dream, rocking herself.*)

(*Looks up*) Yes, Lord, I am listening, yes. What is that you say, Lord? Yes, blessed be your holy name. Yes, I will wash, immediately. Thank you for the gift of water that followed me in my exile. How I love the water . . . (*She moves, kneels, and makes the motions of washing her hands, face, and legs.*) How good the water feels on my skin. (*She looks at herself and stands up, half laughing, half crying.*) Oh, Oh, Oh, I cannot stop laughing.

So that is all it was. How good the water felt on my skin. The moment it touched me the sickness left. "I sing to the Lord for he has triumphed gloriously." I always knew there was laughter in the Lord.

So that is all it was, a divine joke to scare Moses and Aaron, to teach *me?* (*She pauses and thinks; a sly look comes to her face.*) How funny to think that it scared Aaron; he must have feared it would happen to him also, this sickness on the skin. But he need not fear. Aaron does not know this kind of jealousy. It scared Moses, too. How fervently he prayed when the Lord punished me. It made this motley crew wait for me; without water they wait for seven days. And here I am whole again.

It was not Moses' pleading that healed me, was it, Lord? No, I know what it was. (*Her face changes, full of understanding and kindness.*) Mercy for my jealousy, forgiveness like the cool healing water on the rotting skin. Blessed be the name of the Lord.

And now I must return to them. Seven days shut out of camp, seven days to think, to pray, to understand. Seven good days of peace. Now I must return to the noise of the camp, to people quarreling and screaming at Moses, to those who want to fight, and to those who want peace. I must return to Moses and Aaron with my forgiveness. It is for them, too, that this has happened, but I will not explain. Men do not understand what women feel about their God. Let Moses think it was he who healed me; let Aaron think he was not punished because he did not sin.

*(She wraps herself in her shawl and starts to leave. Pauses.)*

Yet, O Lord, generations hence, when people still will call you blessed, the question will echo through women's wombs: Why did the Lord punish Miriam and not Aaron? Why? And only I will know the secret.

## Questions to Ponder

1. Why did the Lord punish Miriam and not Aaron? What is your opinion?

2. Does it bother you that Miriam is punished in this way? She was, after all, one of the three leaders in the wilderness. Why would her role be any less than that of Aaron?

3. Can you enter into the mind of this woman who has the tender memory of Moses' early years and her role in them? Can you then identify with the aging leader who is cast out and not defended by this brother

whom she had helped rescue? What would your feelings be in such a situation? How does one find the strength to rise above resentment?

4. In the monologue, what is Miriam's secret and how does she gradually come to an understanding of her role and her relationship to the Lord?

# NINE

# God of Our Mothers

## RUTH GIVES HER LEGACY TO OBED

**All of the book of Ruth**

*(At harvest time Ruth and Obed are watching the reapers.)*

Hidden in the alien corn, I wept. So this is what my life has become, I thought. The end of love, the end of dreams, the end of promise. Gleaning for what the reapers let drop or do not have the energy to pick for themselves. Living off what others throw away.

I straightened up for just a moment from the back-breaking work. The blond wheat caught the rays of the early sun and glistened gold, the pointed little arrows loaded with seeds weaving gently in the morning breeze. It was a sight to fill the heart with joy: It would be a rich harvest. Instead, tears blurred my vision, and all the gold became a liquid pain running down my face. I was a stranger among strangers, an alien in a foreign land. *(She smiles at her son, but her eyes are filled with tears.)*

I, who had been Ruth the proud Moabitess—Ruth the lovely, they called me at home, a prize catch for any man, my father had said. But I had loved the Hebrew boy, had loved him with all the strength of my young heart and had gone against my father's wishes when I married him.

So my friend Orpah and I married the two Ephrathites from Bethlehem. We of Moab chose to marry them while they were in our land, and we became the wives of two proud foreigners and daughters to Elimelech and Naomi. They were strong and different, our husbands, and Naomi wore the love of all four of her children like a crown.

And then it struck—the illness that snatched them from us. First Elimelech from Naomi, and then Mahlon and Chilion from us, cut down like the wheat stalks in front of me right now are cut by reapers' scythes.

All three of us were left widowed—Naomi, Orpah, and me—and there was no longer any meaning to our lives. Good, wise Naomi, so beautiful, so proud, was suddenly a broken old woman. "I was full and now I am empty," she kept saying, until I thought the refrain would break my heart, and I swore to do all in my power to give her some comfort.

*(Ruth now tells a very familiar story. Her faithfulness is already legendary but she tells it as though it is something ordinary.)*

After the terrible first days of mourning had passed, Naomi said, "Let us go to the fields, my daughters, I need to talk to you."

I noticed that she carried a bag under her garments and a suspicion hit me. Quickly I slipped behind and loaded what few possessions and clothes I had and hid them under my cloak. I had already made up my mind.

And it came to pass as I suspected. She gave us her blessing and sent us home. She said what we had heard all our lives. "We are women alone, and women without men are nothing. I, my daughters," she said, "have no hope of another son for you to marry so you too can have the hope of sons someday. Go with my blessings back to your people so you can marry and have sons and be somebody again."

I let Orpah do the farewell weeping. She kissed Naomi and went back to her people. Orpah was always smart. She knew how to do what was expected of her. Her parents would take her back. Naomi looked at me and waited for me to do the same. "I am empty, Ruth," she said again. "I have nothing to give you. Don't make yourself a nobody like me." (*Ruth shakes her head. Her generation is moving beyond such thinking.*)

I remembered her son, the husband I had loved; all the stories he had told me about his God came back to me. He was not always an attractive God, but there was something in the stories that had captured my loyalty. Yahweh was a trustworthy God who cared for his people, and his people were the Israelites. I wanted to be one of them.

"Your people shall be my people," I told Naomi, "and your God my God. Where you go, I will go; where you die, I will die." And then I swore before the Lord that I would not go back on my word; only death would part us. She tried to talk me out of it, but I saw that some of the emptiness had left her face, and I knew I had chosen well. We started out on the long journey together.

I am sure she would have died on that terrible journey had she not wanted to see that I survived. Thus we survived together. Women can do anything together, but on that I could never get Naomi to agree. (*She smiles at her son. This is strange to his ears, but she is sure of her truth.*)

And so we came to the gates of my new home—Bethlehem. There I stood, a poor widow, with a poor widowed mother-in-law, standing in the alien corn.

I could not watch Naomi shrivel up with hunger. I remembered my husband telling me about the law of his God and how mercy was shown to the poor and the migrants, how the whole field would not be gleaned in reaping, so that something was left for the poor to pick. I too became one of the poor—frightened of my being a foreigner, scared of the young men looking at me with eyes I had never before encountered, shy before the other maidens who followed the reapers.

I stood there, sick for home, wondering why I had not gone back to my parents to live a normal life. With tears blurring my eyes I prayed: "Oh God of my dead husband, God of Naomi, protector of the poor, protector of the widows and of the stranger, save me from shame, keep me from despair, make me a comfort to Naomi."

And I can tell you with all truthfulness, my beloved son, that our God answered me. (*Her son is troubled and she comforts him with better memories.*)

Your father came to my rescue that day, your good, loving father, whose kindness engulfed me from the very first time he saw me, as he told me later, sad and modest, following the reapers, gleaning his fields.

It was your good grandmother Naomi who taught me how to follow the customs of this land and how to remind Boaz, your father, of his relationship to her. He could have rejected me or shamed me when, washed and anointed and in the bloom of my womanhood, I lay at his feet as he slept on the threshing floor. He stirred in the night and found me there, but did not shame me. What I never told him was the sheer terror that lay with me that night until he spoke in kindness to me. Generous in his heart, he agreed to protect me, and today here I am, an honored wife with a beautiful son, with Naomi enjoying a graceful old age, and with a special knowledge in my heart. (*She pauses. She has told her story. But now Obed wants to hear more.*)

You want to know what that is? Good. This is why I have called you to me today, my son. I want to tell you myself that men misinterpret our God's commands. He is not only the God of Israel; he is the God of all who seek him. Otherwise, why would I be so blessed? (*She persists, despite her son's surprise.*)

I have already told you that the stories my first husband, Chilion, taught me back in Moab made me interested in the God of Israel, but I did not always find that God attractive. There was too much killing, too much revenge attributed to Yahweh. There was fear and hatred of foreigners in those stories and more revenge yet. But even though I listened carefully, I wondered about those stories.

How can some of the orders of this strange God be true when his fine people, Naomi and Elimelech and their two sons, can show mercy to women of Moab and marry us and live in harmony? I wanted to find the answer, the truth, for myself. I followed Naomi to this chosen land of the chosen people. And I learned what I, a poor woman, had surmised in my heart: Men do not know all there is to know of our God. For their own selfishness and arrogance and greed they make war and then they say, God told us to do so. But my heart knows a God who is merciful and just and not vindictive. (*This is startling news to her son. He needs to think about all this.*)

And so, my son, this I shall teach you to carry as your heritage: Naomi's loyalty and Boaz's love taught me that the God of Israel is trustworthy and merciful to Israelites and foreigners alike. We are all his chosen people when we are obedient. This I leave you as my legacy. (*She puts both hands on her son's head.*)

Look how God answered my prayer and protected me and brought me to honor. And now, my beloved son, as I look at you, I am convinced that God has great things in store for you. Only God knows what honor you and your descendants will bring to my name.

## Questions to Ponder

1. The writer of the Book of Ruth is very honest about the lust and dangers that surrounded the young widow when she was out in the fields. This is an ancient story, but how much has since changed for unprotected, poor women?

2. How much courage did it take for Ruth to follow Naomi's advice about sleeping at Boaz's feet? Do you find this picture degrading? Why or why not?

3. In the monologue, Ruth says, "Women can do anything together," something Naomi—who cannot think of life without the support of a man—does not understand. Are you a Naomi or a Ruth? And how do you relate with your opposites?

# Will Israel Ever Learn?

## TAMAR CONFRONTS HER FATHER, KING DAVID

### 1 Samuel 13–19; 1 Kings 1:1–2:10

*(Tamar finally tells her terrible story.)*

So, King David, here we are, the two of us. I cannot ever call you father. You were king, and you were lord, and to your sons you were father, but to us, the girls, you were never father. The distant king, the victorious warrior, the lover of other men's wives, but never my own father. *(She looks at the mount of covers on the bed and finally sees his face.)*

Ach, look at you. You are a withered shell of a man lying there in that royal bed, empty now of the young Abishag, the Shunammite who comes to warm your ancient bones in vain. Miserable girl, she is a beauty now, almost as beautiful as I was once. I, Tamar, your daughter, Tamar the beauty, beautiful Absalom's sister. Doesn't it grieve you sometimes? You lost your two most beautiful children. You mourned for Absalom, but never for me, yet I am just as dead. You open your eyes and look at me. You do not know me. Can you perhaps hear me?

(*She waits. She is very nervous.*) I sent the Shunammite out to get some rest, to go see her family—miserable child, chosen by men to lie with you day and night. What a fate. Almost as sad as mine. I promised Bathsheba that I would sit with you while Abishag is gone.

(*Bitterly*) I wonder, do you notice that Bathsheba herself doesn't enter your room? Why should she? Royal wealth and treatment have kept her comely still, so she has no need to come warm the bones of an old man. I don't blame her. She has her Solomon, your heir, and that is all she desires now. To become the mother of the king.

Everyone wants something from you, except for me that is. What I wanted once upon a time—my dignity, my virgin youth, my life—you let your son take from me, and you never told me you were sorry for me. You never told me. How can I call you Father? (*She is surprised to find herself weeping.*)

Ach, even now, after all the dryness and the bitterness, the tears come. Do you remember what I was, what I looked like on that fateful day you sent for me to go to your firstborn, the hated Amnon, cursed be his memory? As humble as I was, I knew enough to see myself as beautiful. I was, after all, Absalom's mirror image. Ah, I see you stir when I mention his name. Can you hear me, King David?

I could see that Absalom's beauty was near perfection. Do you remember that hair, like a young lion's mane, blond, full, and heavy like gold and fate? Do you remember the skin without a flaw? Mine was covered with long sleeves and long robes, but it was flawless also. And no man had ever seen it. How I longed for the sweet love of a good young man those days. Absalom and I thought we were privileged because the Lord had chosen to bestow such comeliness on us, the children of your wife Maacah. Nothing could touch us. We glowed in each other's presence. Knowing smiles passed between us. Absalom was troubled at first because he was not the firstborn, but everyone loved him. They looked at him and loved him, so he had no doubt that good things would befall him. All I wanted was to be your good daughter, King David, to obey you and to live my life in honor, adoring you and my brother. (*The good memories are gone. Now the terror returns.*)

And then that monster sent for me. I was so proud at first. I thought, Amnon, the firstborn, is sick and I am chosen to give him his food, to make him love life again. Did you not guess his motives? You had experience, you who seduced Bathsheba. But what did I know of men's lust? What did I know of evil? I had lived my life sheltered in the palace, a precious sister to my brother, and you sent me to that corrupt young man who knew nothing of honor.

I remember his feverish eyes upon me as I kneaded the dough, made the fire, and baked the cakes. I started burning. I thought, I have come too close to the fire. Something oppressive was upon me, but I did not know what it was. *I did not know!* He burned me with his lust, and I did not know what it was.

But still, I did not feel threatened. The room had servants in it; I was not alone. And then he sent them all out. I wanted to scream, to say, "Don't leave me! I am frightened." But something in me said, "Would my father, King David, have sent me to danger? Why am I afraid?" *(With irony and now anger.)* Do you hear, old man, why I am so angry with you? *Would* you have sent me to danger? *Did* you send me to danger and disgrace? He was my half brother, wasn't he? He would not harm me. Is that what you thought? But could you not see how sick in his mind he was when he begged you for me? Could you not see?

*(She is telling this story for the first time. The horror is still present.)*

I kept my eyes downcast through the whole ordeal. I did not want to look at him. And when he called me into his bedchamber, I thought, "I will put these before him, and I will leave. Something here does not feel right." And then his hand grabbed me by the arm, and I was lost. The fear threatened to choke me. Even then I had sense enough to know what was right. I did not panic. I thought I could reason with him. "Do not do this thing, my brother," I begged. I called him "my brother." I wanted him to remember who I was, but the evil was in him. "Do not do anything so vile," I begged. And then I remembered that in Israel I could marry him, my half brother. I appealed to him, "Ask the king; he will give me to you in marriage. Do not disgrace me; do not make yourself one of the scoundrels of Israel." But he kept pulling me to his bed, and I fought him. I knew then, that if I had had the strength, I would have killed him. But I was only a girl, with slender arms that had done nothing strenuous since birth. And he, the stronger, the vile man, took me and raped me. *(Her voice rises.)*

Hear the word, father of Amnon. He raped me. I lost all that was sacred to me. My honor, my youth, my virginity, my beauty. He grabbed them from me; he robbed me of all honor. Even then, I thought, through my tears, the blood, and the excruciating pain, he will now do the right thing. King David did not beget a monster. Until I saw him turn away from me as though I were unclean. "Get out!" he screamed. Then I knew that I was dead. But I was a king's daughter; I could not let him throw me out like a common prostitute. "Please, my brother," I begged, "do not do this to me. For this is worse than your taking me against my will. This is a terrible wrong; don't do it." But even my humiliation and my begging would not persuade him. His loathing was stronger than his lust had been. I was then really frightened both for me and for him, for I saw him dead. He could not survive after what he had done to me. How could he? (*Mocking her father*) The king would not let him live. Would you, King David? Would you have punished your darling Amnon?

And then he called his servant and ordered him to throw me out and to bolt the door after me, as though I had been the thief and he the victim. (*Harshly*) Are you hearing me, King David? When the servant threw me out something terrible happened to my heart, which had been filled with love for all before that moment. I wanted to see Amnon dead. I had never before and have never since felt the desire to see someone dead. He was my murderer, and I wanted him dead.

(*He knows all this, but she wants him to hear it from her own lips.*)

Since I felt dead, I wanted the world to know it also. I took the ashes from the fire that I had built in such innocence a few hours before and put them on my head. I tore my lovely robe, the remnant of my virgin youth, to shreds, covered my head with my hand, and stumbled, wailing in the yard. I did not know where to go. I was blinded with tears, desolate with shame. There was nowhere for me to go. I was disgraced. A daughter of Israel who is raped and thrown out can only wait for the stoning. The fault lies with her, not with her violator. Don't you find that strange and cruel, just king? You were just to some people, weren't you, King David? Think of the mercy you showed to Jonathan's grandson. Remember how again and again you spared the life of Saul, your tormentor, back when you were young and your thoughts were pure? (*Even now, she appeals to him like a child.*)

Why did you not come to my rescue when I stumbled in the palace courtyard crying? I thought for a moment that it was your arm that had gone around my shoulders when I stumbled and fell, but it was my darling Absalom who lifted me and asked, "Has your brother Amnon been with you, my sister?" I nodded dumbly, unable to accept the word "brother" coupled with the hated name. I finally lifted my eyes and looked at Absalom. He was deathly pale and very quiet. His words were strangely calm coming out of those lips that were set in an ominous kind of control. He said, so that the rest, all the men who gathered around to stare, could hear, "Hush, be quiet for now, my sister; do not take all this so to heart. He is your brother, after all." I started to scream at him too, but then I heard him, "Be quiet for now, my sister." For now. I would do it for Absalom. What did it matter? I was already dead, and there was no one else to help me. So Absalom led me to his house, and there I hid for years, waiting for justice. (*She and Absalom had different understandings of justice.*)

I am still waiting, and many years have gone by. I knew Absalom would kill him eventually, but I did not know how long it would take him to act. I did not think that Absalom had it in him to be patient. And I never guessed in those years how much he had come to despise you, his father. It all started with my disgrace; did you know that, King David? I, Tamar, the hidden daughter, the unclean and defiled daughter, caused the beginning of the crumbling of your kingdom. How strange, do you not think so? Did you, in the dark of night, wonder how different your kingdom would have been had you punished Amnon immediately after he disgraced me? Have you agonized at night? Have you asked yourself what happened to turn your darling Absalom into an enemy?

It was I, Tamar, your daughter. (*With bitter satisfaction*) Think about it now. The daughter you gave no mind to after the disgrace caused the fall of the house of David. For that is what happened. I don't care how many victories you have had since then, and how you may think that your God has blessed you; after the death of Absalom, nothing has been the same. Nothing. And none of us thinks differently. Don't listen to your sycophants. The end came when you let Absalom die. Oh, I know you mourned him. But it was too late, King David. Too late. You should have gone to him immediately after my disgrace. You should have known he would kill Amnon after what that monster did to me. There are some men who love women for more than their bodies. Do you not know this? Absalom loved me. My pain became his. He longed for justice for all. He did not find it in you, so he decided to punish you, his father. Oh Absalom, my brother.

*(She is lost in her grief. Some time passes.)*

Do I feel better now that I have let you know of my hatred and pain? Do I feel anything seeing you as a wrinkled, dried up shell of a man? Ach, I would like to feel nothing, but something is stirring in my heart, seeing you so helpless. Do you suppose I am not dead after all? For how many years have I hidden in Absalom's house? I can no longer count. Strange how all that I had heard about your God has stayed with me. How many times I have wondered, what do these men know about God? Is it true what they say about the God of Abraham, Isaac, and Jacob? Are they now going to add your name to the list?

*(She stands up and moves close to the bed and looks at his face.)*

I have thought again and again of all that was good in Absalom, of his beauty, his thirst for justice, which was greater than his thirst for power—I don't think you knew that—and I have wondered how God would let him perish. But suddenly I remembered that it was your general who killed him, not your God, and I want to tell this to all the people of Israel: How little you know about your God! And it is this that makes me want to forgive you now, King David. You open your eyes and look at me. Are those tears falling on your pillow? Is it possible that you know how deeply you hurt me? *(With resignation)* I will let you go. I think you have heard me. That is enough.

May you find peace in Sheol. I don't want you to be tormented anymore. Go in peace, my father.

*(She catches her breath. She straightens her shoulders. For the first time, she smiles.)*

Ah, how good that felt. I long to tell the people of Israel that forgiveness feels much better than hatred. Will they ever learn? Will they?

## Questions to Ponder

1. Often, when we are hurt by another, we keep our pain to ourselves. What do you think of Tamar telling her father about her injury? Has there been a time in your life when confronting someone changed something about your life?

2. On page 90 Tamar tells of her feelings of shame about being raped, and of society's view that the rape was her fault rather than Amnon's. How much has that view changed since biblical times? Are there other things, besides rape, for which women tend to bear the shame when it belongs elsewhere?

3. What does Tamar gain by forgiving King David? Why does she do it? Does forgiveness imply that we are willing to be hurt by that person in the same way again?

4. Would you have forgiven King David? Why or why not?

# ELEVEN

# Is He Only a God of War?

## MICHAL PUZZLES THE QUESTION

**1 Samuel 9–2 Samuel 6**

*(Michal, David's wife, tells her story to Tamar, David's daughter, as the two women walk in the walled garden of the palace.)*

Now, Tamar, you listen to me. There are worse things in life than living without love. The death of love tastes more bitter still. You talk of your father, David. I want to tell you about my lover, David, my erstwhile husband. You listen to me and remember. Don't see me as the old crone I am now. Remember that I also was young once, and almost as lovely as you were before the fateful day. *(Michal removes her headscarf, defiant in old age.)*

It was another life, another time. We were all in King Saul's court those days. You should have seen my father before the madness came upon him. He stood taller than all the men of Israel, my handsome, crazy father. I thought him glorious. And it was *your* father who brought him down. His children, Jonathan and I, Michal, helped him to do so. I have never forgiven myself. I'll tell you the story and you judge. And maybe then you'll stop feeling so sorry for yourself, Tamar. Come here. Sit with me. It is a long story. (*They sit together and Michal is happy. She loves to tell stories.*)

Saul, the first king, my father, was a man among men. Tall, good looking, willing to please, easy to love and be loved. He was ruled by his emotions and by Samuel. Have you heard of Samuel, the mad prophet? First he chooses my father to be king and then he withdraws the choosing. And not willingly. He didn't anoint him willingly, but he grieved when he withdrew the anointing. He didn't want Israel to have a king, and then, when he anointed Saul, he kept saying that God told him to withdraw the favor. It was enough to drive a stable man mad, and Saul was none too stable. He wanted to please God by pleasing Samuel, but he always ended up doing things that Samuel said God didn't like. I reached the point of hating this up-and-down God-favor. It destroyed my father.

(*She listens to Tamar's question.*)

Yes, I know, I said David destroyed him, not God. But sometimes it is hard to know which is which. When my father was anointed king, we were little then, Jonathan and I, and very confused about what it all meant. Mostly, for us, it meant war. Our father was always gone, fighting, killing one enemy after the other, so we didn't know him very well. By the time we were old enough to know what was going on, he was in God's disfavor. Or so old Samuel said. (*She shrugs. This is a bitterness she has carried for a lifetime.*)

Whenever Saul was in the palace, a darkness would descend upon him. He tolerated only Jonathan, his favorite son. The rest of us were like acquaintances to him, but still, for all his children, the king was a glorious sight. We peeked through the drapes just to see his great height, that big noble head and the proud bearing. But we were also afraid of him. We never knew when he would start throwing things. So we hid and watched.

And that is how I came to see David. Abner had brought him to the palace, telling Saul that this was a gifted singer and player on the lyre, and he would soothe Saul's wounded spirit. What Saul did not know then was that Samuel had already anointed David to be his successor. But I must give credit to David for this. He never acted toward Saul as if this anointing had taken place. He served my father well. Saul loved him at first. He made him his armor bearer, and David went everywhere with him. And when darkness sat on Saul's brow, David would play and sing, and all was well for a while. (*Her youthful memories are good. Her eyes are sparkling.*)

David was a lovely sight. I stood behind the drape for hours looking at him. His curly hair was gold-red and fell on a high forehead. His skin was always burnished by the sun, but it was his eyes that held me—me and everyone else, now that I think about it. Even Saul was affected. As long as he looked at David's beautiful eyes, he seemed well. For David sang of life. He described in his songs all the earth's loveliness. Saul would court death in his dark days, but David would call him back to life, and me to love, thought he didn't know it. I could have died for him then. And I was sure that Jonathan felt the same. I have lived a long time, but I have never seen a friendship like theirs. Most of the love was on Jonathan's part. David seemed used to being loved. That voice and those eyes seduced everyone. But Jonathan was the one who knew how to love. My lovely brother had no self interest. Of how many men can we say this?

Whom do you know that would give a kingdom for a friend? Even your beloved Absalom could never reach that height. Jonathan did not know the meaning of jealousy. Time and again Saul tried to kill David, but Jonathan saved David's life. Jonathan would warn him, put his own life in danger, betray his father just to save David. (*She pauses and takes a deep breath.*) I must be fair. David did not ask him to do this. Jonathan offered, and David accepted. But in this friendship, it was Jonathan who excelled, who set standards no one else has even approached. Jonathan loved David as his own soul.

It was David's great victory over Goliath that finally shook Saul's confidence, and from that day on he set out to get rid of the upstart. After that great adventure, I knew I could not live without David. Decked out in Jonathan's robe and armor, David returned triumphant from the battle, and I and all the girls ran toward him singing, "Saul has killed his thousands, and David his ten thousands." That was the beginning of the end for Saul.

One minute Saul would be full of love and admiration for David, then he would throw his spear at the boy to kill him. Immediately, he would regret it and beg David to come back. He was at his worst when he was sly. He tried to marry him off to my older sister, Merab, but before David could make up his mind, she was married to someone else. I decided that I had to let him know that I loved David, and I would marry him. So I told Jonathan,

"Please tell my father to give me as wife to David."
Jonathan, who knew Saul better than the rest of us, was
very hesitant. "He will agree," he told me, "but wait and
see. Saul will extract some heavy price for you."

Of course, Jonathan was right. It would be funny if it
had not been so gruesome. Saul demanded a hundred
foreskins for me, so David had to kill and despoil a hun-
dered Philistines before he could marry me. So, instead of
life, it was death that brought us together. (*She stops and
thinks about what she has just said. Only when Tamar asks
her to continue does she begin again.*)

After the marriage, Saul became more and more afraid
of David and the succession. And David had victory after
victory in battle. One night, a few months after our marriage, I heard David running to the house. I opened the
door and rushed with him upstairs. "Your father tried to
kill me tonight," he said. "His spear barely missed me." I
bathed him and gave him supper and then we went to
bed. David fell asleep immediately, but I stayed awake,
listening. Underneath the window I heard voices. Saul's
men had arrived and they sat around the house waiting
for dawn. I heard enough of their talk to know that in the
morning they would capture David, and that would be
the end. So I went downstairs and offered them something to drink and eat, so that they would all come to the
front of the house. Then I ran back upstairs and shook
David awake. "Don't talk; get ready. Saul has sent his people to kill you. Leave while it is dark. Save your life." I
knew that I would probably never see him again. But I
loved him, and I wanted him to live. So while the men ate
my food, I helped David jump from the window and dis-

appear into the night. *(She puts her hand on Tamar's own. She does not like the memory she is about to share.)*

And it was then that I learned to deceive. I took a wooden idol I had, a work of pagan art that I had hidden from David and from Saul, and put it on the bed and covered it. Then I made hair out of goats' wool and waited. As soon as light broke, the men called for David. I went to the door. "Shhhh . . . he is sick," I told them and showed them the bed. They went back to Saul to give the news. And Saul, in all his madness, said to them, "Go bring him on the bed, so I can kill him." I decided I had done enough harm to the men, so I went with them. There they were, carrying this bed with the idol on it to the king of Israel. Saul was furious at me. "Why did you do this to me? You let my enemy go! You deceived me." It was too late to try to explain that David was not the enemy. So I continued my deception. "He made me do it," I answered. "He asked me to let him go. He did not want to kill me."

From that day on, madness led to madness. Saul became obsessed with killing David, and Jonathan was just as determined to save him. The two friends met frequently and wept together, knowing that their past friendship, in the familiar surroundings of the palace, could never be. By that time, Jonathan knew that David would be king and not he himself, but even that knowledge did not turn him from David. But it infuriated Saul. To spite David and Jonathan, he gave me as wife to Paltiel, a sweet young man who became one more victim in this story.

*(She reacts to Tamar's surprise at the revelation.)*

Did I object? What a question. What difference would

it have made? David was gone. I had heard of his other wives and the children they bore him. When I saved his life that night, I knew he was no longer mine. Little by little, the kindness of my new husband, his devotion to me, and the peace of our life together comforted me. And suddenly, it seemed, both Jonathan and Saul were dead. David was still at large, with most of Israel his devoted followers. It was only a matter of time.

This is where Abner comes back into the story. Abner was a kingmaker, but very different from Samuel. He was insulted by one of my half brothers and, knowing that David was the strong one, went to offer his services to the new king. Once more I became a thing to be played with. David, all of a sudden, remembered me. He agreed to see Abner, but only if I was returned to him. After all, he bragged, he had paid a hundred foreskins for me! So Abner came to our house. He didn't ask; he simply gave the orders: "King David has sent for you. You are still married to him, and you must follow me."

That was that. Paltiel, who loved me, fell on his knees and held me. "Don't go, Michal. Don't go." Tell me, Tamar, what can a woman do in such a case? Where is our power? Well, you know all about that, don't you?

*(The two women hold each other and weep.)*

Abner waited outside while we said our good-byes, and I left with few of my belongings. But Paltiel would not accept the separation. He walked behind me, weeping the whole time. My heart was breaking for him. I started feeling an anger toward David that has never left me. What right had he to do this to Paltiel, a young innocent man who had never harmed anyone? No matter that David was king to most of Israel, I did not grant him that right. I walked on with my head down, listening to my husband's sobs behind me, and I hardened my heart and vowed that I would never love anyone again. Men are unjust to one another. I didn't even try to think then about how unjust they are to us, the women.

*(She stands up and starts pacing.)*

When we reached Bahurim, Abner turned on Paltiel and ordered him back home. I watched his poor shape disappear into the twilight and felt such sorrow and such bitterness that there was no joy left about seeing David again.

Abner, of course, paid for all of this with his own life, but that is another story. I became a member of a household full of women and children. I longed for my life with Paltiel, as the only beloved wife of a good man. But all of that was finished. I had been David's first wife, so all the maids looked to me for orders. David was gone most of the time doing what he loved best, fighting.

*(She sits down and looks at Tamar, who is full of interest.)*

The death of love came when he returned from bringing back the ark. Have you heard that story? Yes, I can see you have. They say that is why I never bore a child. Ha! I'll tell you what happened. David was returning with his men and with the ark, sacrificing oxen and making such a huge celebration that the trumpets sounded from far away, and all of us went to the windows and the roofs to look out. And soon, what do I see? There is King David, naked, with just an ephod[5] around his loins, dancing and

---

5. A cloth worn around the loins.

singing and jumping up and down around the ark, with people following him like a crowd of drunks. I remembered suddenly the boy he used to be, the lovely youngster who sang so sweetly with the lyre as accompaniment, and I missed that sweetness of youth that hadn't yet learned to kill. And I knew that moment that I despised the man before me, the king who danced naked, who was always triumphant in battle. I saw the girls hiding behind their scarves and laughing. I was embarrassed.

He fed the people with the meat of the sacrificed oxen, and then he started to come to us. I ran out to meet him. I wanted him to know that I despised him. You see what I mean, Tamar? The death of love is a bitter thing. I lashed out at him. "You shamed yourself," I told him. "You uncovered yourself like a vulgar nobody. I was ashamed before all the maids."

He looked at me, but he did not become angry. He said it was all because he rejoiced in his Lord. "I don't mind being shamed," he said. "I will become contemptible even as long as I honor my Lord." I no longer understood him. I don't know what men mean when they talk about their God. All I knew then was that I was sick of war and the honor they gave to God for their victories. I shut myself in my room and made it clear that I did not want him to come in to me.

(*She pats Tamar's hand. Then she takes the end of her shawl and wipes the younger woman's tears.*)

And so our love died forever. I did not want any sons that would grow up to become warriors and killers. I had enough of that with my father. War killed my brother Jonathan, and David gloried in war so much that he would dance naked before the Lord. It baffles me still.

*(She has made a decision.)* Listen, Tamar. The time has come for us women to try to understand who the God of Israel is and what it is that pleases him. Can it be war and killing? What has it brought to David? Look at his sorrow with his sons. So many dead, so many killed. What is it that makes us different from the pagans? Let us, you and I, think on this together, my child.

## Questions to Ponder

1. At the beginning of the monologue, Michal tells Tamar that there are worse things than living without love. She says that the death of love is worse than not having love in the first place. What do you think of that statement?

2. Michal is constantly at the beck and call of the men in her life in this story. She must get her father's permission to marry, and she is pulled in and out of marriages at the whim of the men around her. Women today still experience the same problem many times. Have you had experiences of this kind? How do you handle them?

# TWELVE

# *My Name Is Not Israel*

## GOMER'S ACCOUNT OF HER STORY IN TWO PARTS

**All of the book of Hosea, especially chapters 1–3**

### 1. The early years
*(an interior monologue as she waits to be sold into slavery)*

*(Gomer, her clothes torn, her eyes burning, is sitting on the ground in the marketplace. Across from her, a crowd of men jeers.)*

I am tired of being forgiven. I am tired of being mistaken for a nation. I am just a woman, quite bad in everyone's eyes, but a woman nonetheless, a wife and a mother. That's all. Hosea thinks I am a nation. He calls me Israel.

He decided that he had to rescue me, which was fine with me, but a person gets tired of being rescued and of being good. I wanted only to be left alone, not to be reminded of who I was when he found me. Look at them. They are standing there waiting to stone me or to sell me. But I know all of them so well. I want to yell at them:

"None of you is good enough to stone me! You will do it anyway, but I want you to know that you are not good enough. You are just as bad as I am, if you would only admit it. Worse I think. You made me who I am." And who am I? A woman refusing to be a nation. A thing despised, sitting in the marketplace, waiting to be sold. Has all my life led me to this?

I was still quite young when Hosea first found me. He came seeking a wife among the temple prostitutes. Right away that should have given me a hint that something was wrong with him, but he was determined to rescue me. He didn't bother to ask me why I was where I was; I did not choose to be a harlot. My father sent me out of the house one day, with no food and no money. What was I to do to survive? I went to Baal's priests and there I met my fate. (She is still defiant, but shaken.)

Yet, Hosea gave me his hand and took me home to be his wife. Only, the way he talked about it, it was all very mixed up in his mind. I was Israel, he said, but he, or his heart, was the heart of God. Does that make sense? I was the harlot and he was the savior. He raved in the night. Words poured out of him nonstop. He frightened me with his crazed talk about God loving Israel and being hurt by Israel's whoring and about God's pain at Israel's unfaithfulness. I understood none of it.

But I put up with all of it for a while, because Hosea is a good man. In anybody's judgment, he is a good man. The trouble began when the children came. He named them wild names. One was Jezreel, which means "God sows"; the girl was Lo-ruhamah, which means "Not pitied"—can you believe that?—and the third was Lo-ammi, which means "Not my people." Well, I did not like it; I tell you that. And even though he was tender with them, and he would lift up the babies and hold them close and bend down to them and feed them, he started saying they were not his. *(She is now very agitated thinking of her children. For the first time, tears fill her eyes.)*

All of this came to him from God, he said. When I heard him talking to his God and asking what he would do about the children, I knew I had to get out. I also knew that if I left the children with him they would come to no harm. I went back to doing what I knew. My lovers were glad to have me back, and they did not talk to God all day and all night, even though they considered themselves priests of their god, Baal. My old life came naturally to me, but I longed for my babies and even missed the kindness of Hosea. Still, it is very hard to live with a good man who constantly reminds you that he forgave you. I was more comfortable being my familiar bad self.

*(She looks at the jeering crowd and her monologue is no longer interior.)* That is when you so-called upright men decided to punish me for my wickedness. But don't I recognize you? Haven't I seen you in the fertility rites around the statues of Baal? Come, come, you may wear masks of decency, but I would know you anywhere. Yet, here I am like a common animal, waiting for the slaughter.

*(She is puzzled. Looks around.)* What is this? Why do you turn away? Is this Hosea I see coming through the crowd?

## 2. *The later years*
### *(as she recounts them to her daughter)*

*(Gomer is shy with her daughter at first. Gradually, she becomes more confident.)*

You have heard terrible words about your mother, but you must learn what changed me. I was about to lose my life when Hosea came and rescued me again. I still wasn't certain that I wanted to be rescued, but I had reached the lowest point of my miserable life. Even so, I had spunk. "Hosea," I asked, "are you mistaking me for Israel again?" "No," he said, "no, Gomer, I know who you are. My poor, lost wife. The wife I love. Come back to me and the children, Gomer. Stay with me and learn to love as I have loved you. Be my wife and I will be your husband."

Imagine telling a harlot you love her. How could I turn away from such love? He no longer seemed ashamed of me. He put a cloak on my back to cover me and walked with me among those horrid, leering men and took me home.

*(She pauses. Finally she responds to a kind prompt from her daughter.)* So many years have passed. You, our children, are now grown, and you survived all my mistakes and your father's fervor. Hosea and I are growing old together. He has been a different man since he found me and brought me back. He stopped confusing me with a nation. When he brought me home the second time, he treated me kindly and with fewer words. He let me be. I was like an honored guest for a long while, do you remember? We did not live like husband and wife. He allowed me to rest and to learn. I finally understood something of what he was trying to do for Israel. And I

learned to pity him. He is a man so full of love and kindness, but he is not listened to by the people. He tried to tell them that God had made a covenant with them, that they had dishonored the covenant, and that God, who is just, would drive them out of his house. But they will not listen. Seeing his pain, I understood that this is what our marriage was to him, a covenant, a contract, and that I had dishonored our contract. I vowed that it would never happen again. My old ways are gone forever.

After the vow, Hosea became my husband again. He said to me, "You see, my wife, God is just, but he is also forgiving." "Like you?" I asked. He looked at me searchingly and said, "No, God can never be like a man. God is like himself. I am only a vessel." And then he wrote down these words and taught them to me. (*She quotes words long familiar; she has made them her own.*) "How can I give you up, Ephraim? How can I hand you over, O Israel? For I am God and no mortal, the Holy One in your midst, and I will not come in wrath."

I then understood Hosea's heart. He had learned about love that comes from pain. I had caused him pain. Instead of taking revenge on me as other men would have done, he took me back and covered my shame. But this time, having grown in his understanding of God, he did not remind me of my shame. He acted as though it had never happened. That is when I learned to love him. And I learned to love his God. I said to him, "Teach me these words, Hosea. I want to close them in my heart and repeat them night and day. Tell me again about God's heart." He would smile at me then and repeat, "Hold fast to love and justice, and wait continually for your God."

I wrote those words on my heart and went about my chores repeating them. And little by little, healing came. The old was washed away. All the evil that men had heaped upon me, the dirt of their lust, was washed away—the way we wash snow away after it melts and becomes dirty here on the highlands of the northern kingdom. All the pain that I had caused myself by leaving my husband and my children became a reminder of forgiveness. I was no longer afraid of forgiveness. I wore it like a garment of honor. Like Hosea, I wanted to go out and tell the people, "Stop sowing the wind and reaping the whirlwind. Sow for yourselves righteousness; reap steadfast love." (*For a moment, she looks like Hosea, passionate and full of conviction. Then she shakes her head.*)

The miracle is this: I learned about righteousness by seeing Hosea's life, hearing his words, observing his life of justice and honor. And I learned about steadfast love from the way he treated me. Taking me into his heart and home twice and staying faithful and loving even when I had abandoned him. That is steadfast love. So I am beginning to know the heart of God by knowing Hosea. But he, how did he learn about God? He had no one else's example. How is it that some persons are singled out to know the heart of God? It is a mystery.

## Questions to Ponder

1. In the first part of the monologue, why is Gomer so frightened of forgiveness? Have you ever found forgiveness threatening or difficult to accept?

2. Given that Hosea constantly reminded Gomer of his forgiveness of her in the first part of the monologue, do you think he had actually forgiven Gomer? Why or why not?

3. Why is Gomer so angry about being called "Israel"? How do you respond to being seen as a symbol, idol, example, or person to be imitated?

4. Do you think that Gomer is correct about some persons being singled out to know the heart of the will of God? How do you discern God's will in your own life?

# Bibliography

*The Interpreter's Dictionary of the Bible.* Nashville: Abingdon Press, 1962.

*The Questing Spirit: Religion in the Literature of Our Time.* Selected and edited by Halford E. Luccock and Frances Brentano. New York: Coward-McCann, Inc., 1947.

DeVane, William Clyde, ed. *The Shorter Poems of Robert Browning.* New York: Appleton-Century-Crofts, Inc., 1934.

Sayers, Dorothy L. *The Man Born to Be King: A Play-Cycle on the Life of Our Lord and Saviour Jesus Christ.* Grand Rapids: William B. Eerdmans, 1974. (First edition copyright by Dorothy L. Sayers, 1943.)

Sölle, Dorothée, Joe H. Kirchberger, and Herbert Haag. *Great Women of the Bible in Art and Literature.* Macon, Georgia: Mercer University Press, 1994.

Temple, William. *Readings in Saint John's Gospel.* London: Macmillan and Co., Ltd., 1952.

Trible, Phyllis. *Texts of Terror: Literary Feminist Readings of Biblical Narratives.* Philadelphia: Fortress Press, 1984.

9 780819 217585